AFRICAN DOW

AFRICAN DOW

Jim Dow

ATHENA PRESS
LONDON

AFRICAN DOW
Copyright © Jim Dow 2008

All Rights Reserved

ISBN: 978 1 84748 393 5

First published 2008 by
ATHENA PRESS
Queen's House, 2 Holly Road
Twickenham TW1 4EG
United Kingdom

Cover image: Darwin the monkey. See pp.87–92

Printed for Athena Press

To Lorna, Karen, Natasha and Lindsay,
my girls out of Africa.

Into Africa

Telegram from Dar es Salaam to DOW
Start January 4th sports reporter
Tanganyika Standard all fixed
DAD
Received 8.50 a.m. 2nd October 1954

I was aged sixteen when I received that telegram at the Prince of Wales School, Nairobi, Kenya. I read it and reread it time and time again in an effort to get rid of the disbelief and to enjoy as much as possible the message that it conveyed. The next day, according to my diary, I went to see the headmaster and told him: 'My career is settled.'

How right I was. That brief communication from Dad signalled the beginning of a newspaper career which has spanned more than half a century, with five momentous years as a young journalist in East Africa. But the African connection started long before that telegram.

I can't really remember any announcement in our house at Carrick Knowe in Edinburgh to the effect that we were about to uproot ourselves from the land in which we were born and in which we felt more than a little comfortable and settled ('we' being myself and my two younger brothers) to set up house and home in far off Africa.

It was perhaps overshadowed by the death of my grandfather on 26 August 1949 – I attended the funeral in Dunbar, a fishing village and, later, a popular holiday town twenty-eight miles down the east coast from Edinburgh, and held one of the cords attached to my grandfather's coffin, at the age of eleven, along with my father who was 'crying like a bairn' as my diary put it.

By then we knew my father was heading for Africa, with us to follow later, a route not exactly unknown to the Scots. The diary on 29 September 1949, says simply: 'It's Dad's last day.'

The next day he was off to Dar es Salaam in Tanganyika. He

went out by flying boat – one of the last of the flying boat's scheduled passenger trips – and this landed on Lake Naivasha which, as fate would have it, would be on my patch as a scribe for the *East African Standard* many years later.

All I knew was that Dad was going to work for the East African Posts and Telegraphs. I knew there was something of a trial period and, if all went well, we would all follow – Mum and brothers Kelman (nine – I was aged eleven) and Irvin (five). But it had not really sunk in. The event was as far away as Africa itself.

After all, I did have other important matters to take care of. I was the goal-scoring captain of the school football team. I was a star of the future, of that I had no doubt. Sure, I missed my Dad, and would have preferred him to have been on the touchline while I weaved my way through defences at seven in the morning – we had to start early because we were away down on the priority list of pitches which were in constant demand – in freezing weather which snapped at the bare knees and made shivering an art form for the devoted teachers and parents who chastised, cajoled and praised throughout.

The heat of Africa could not have been further from my mind.

Then Dad sent us a coconut. Africa was suddenly in our house at Carrick Knowe. The coconut was still in its husk and Dad had simply red-painted our address on it and sent it off. We sat and stared at it on the living room table. This was not the coconut we had seen in the *Dandy* or *Beano*. This was quite different.

We were learning about Africa already. Africa had arrived in our home in a strange fashion and we were expected to return the compliment fairly soon.

As D for Departure Day loomed closer, I began to panic. It was not the thought of the travel that bothered me – I had, after all, been to Dunbar (twenty-eight miles away) several times and had made one return trip to London, on my own, so I reckoned I was a seasoned traveller – but the final of the Inspector's Cup was imminent and that was more important than any trip to Africa.

There was also a bit of panic about some of the more practical aspects involved in going to this strange land. Did you have to wear football boots in Africa? What about my stamp collection – could I take it with me? What sort of school would I go to? What sort of guys would be there? I also had a great collection of Hibs and Hearts football programmes – would they be wanted in the new world of Africa?

Decisions, decisions, big ones for a wee lad, and I have to admit I gave most of the stuff away. You could hardly keep it all in a mud hut in the jungle. That was the level of mystery about Africa. All we knew about it was from the Tarzan films starring Johnny Weissmuller – I had seen *Tarzan Escapes* eight times so there must have been some African fascination lurking inside J Dow – and it certainly did not look like the place for football boots or a stamp collection. And the coconuts were something else.

We finally said farewell to Scotland, and that glittering football career, on 14 May 1950. I should record that six days earlier we had beaten Abbeyhill 2–1 in the cup final and as team captain I was carried shoulder high so I felt I was going to Africa as a hero.

We left the house by taxi – something in those days used only for funerals and weddings, so we were really starting off in style. I can remember that the neighbours lined the street to say farewell to us. This was a big event. Years later if I bumped into somebody from Carrick Knowe he would search back his childhood memories and say, 'Are you one of the Dows that went to Africa?'

So we were big news. It was a Britain still struggling with the post-war austerity. We were swapping ration books for a passport – only the one, because we were all on Mum's.

The overseas holiday boom and the Costa Espana were years away. Holiday travel then was no more than a few miles down the coast to Portobello or Dunbar. The only people who knew about foreign parts were the Servicemen not long back from the war. And here was a whole family going out to Africa!

We took the train from Edinburgh to London. Mum's brother, Uncle Johnny, was our chaperon. It was not an auspicious start. My diary entry states: 'Today we left Carrick Knowe. We journeyed to London, where we stayed overnight in a hotel. It was good, although we were nearly poisoned by a fish supper.'

Journalistic exaggeration that early on. I can't remember too much about that fish supper, but I do remember the family fears: if this is what the food is like in London, what will it be like in Africa?

There was an incident on the train journey to London which I have not been allowed to forget. I had to use the toilet on the train and that was where I found a used sanitary towel. This was a strange object – remember that I came from a family of three boys – and it looked pretty suspicious to me. So I grabbed hold of it, rushed back to the crowded compartment, held it above my head and shouted: 'Somebody's been murdered!' I have never seen my Uncle Johnny move so quickly.

Our misgivings about the quality of food away from home after the London experience were unfounded. Fortunately, the food was a lot better on board the *Dunnottar Castle* – and there was much more of it. The next day we boarded the vessel at Tilbury after a long wait of four hours. But it got the thumbs up from me: 'It is smashing, good meals, good cabins, my what a luxurious trip.'

The 15,000-ton *Dunnottar Castle*, named after a spectacular Scottish castle in Royal Deeside, was part of the fleet of the Union-Castle Mail Steamship Company Limited. Built by Harland & Wolff in Belfast it was launched in 1936. During the war it had been converted into an armed merchant cruiser by the British Navy.

It was sold in 1958, cruised in Europe and the Caribbean until 1993 with the new name of *Victoria*. It was sold again in 1993, had its name changed to *Princesa Victoria* and was used on cruises to Cyprus when it was the oldest large cruise ship still in passenger service.

It was sold again in 2004 but for the last time because then it headed for the breaker's yard.

But it was not the first *Dunnottar Castle*.

An earlier Union-Castle vessel with the same name had probably taken my maternal grandfather to Africa more than fifty years earlier.

In October 1899, Sir Redvers Buller sailed on the vessel of the same name from Southampton to take command of all the British army forces in South Africa and to win the war against the Boers. My grandfather served under Buller for seven years, including a year in the Boer War, so the chances were that he was on the *Dunnottar Castle* also.

Another passenger on the *Dunnottar Castle* on that journey in 1899 was Winston Churchill, who was going out to cover the war on behalf of the *Morning Post*. Winston went on to be captured by the Boers then made his historic escape and after an eventful nine months sailed home – again on the *Dunnottar Castle*. Lord Kitchener and Lord Roberts also sailed to Africa on the first *Dunnottar*.

So I was obviously in good company. No doubt Buller and Churchill travelled first class on the *Dunnottar* while my grandfather would be roughing it as one of the troops. I certainly did not think we were roughing it – luxury was my word for it.

But I was soon to learn that there were two grades of what I perceived as luxury. We were in Tourist Class. First Class was separate and much better. That did not bother me much, except for the fact that they had an excellent swimming pool in First Class – far better than ours. Ours was made of canvas, which was frequently ripped and the pool would be closed for a day while it was repaired.

However, I was able occasionally to sneak into the First Class pool and sometimes stay quite a while before a steward would recognise me as an interloper from Tourist Class and send me packing.

But while there was a lot more pampering in First Class it cost them more if they did not feel well. In the 'Information for Passengers' there was a section headed 'Medical Attendance' and it stated: 'The Surgeon of this vessel is authorised to charge for professional attendance, inclusive of medicines, at the rate of 10s 0d per visit in the case of First Class passengers and 3s 6d in the case of Tourist Class passengers, with a maximum of two chargeable visits per day.'

That's nearly three times more expensive if you have a First Class illness! I can remember that registering with me, but if I'd been clever I would have done a deal with one of the kids in First Class – you can be sick in my class if you let me swim in yours. But I still had a lot of learning to do.

About deck games, for a start. Deck quoits and deck tennis, for example. Pretty dull, I thought. I was happier in the pool – and at the dining table. No ration books here. The ship's timetable said that at 8 a.m. and 6.30 p.m. there would be a 'dressing gong'. We did not know what it meant but one thing we did know – half an hour later we ate.

The first stop was Gibraltar. I had seen it on stamps and was thrilled to step ashore. Mum fought bravely to keep on the leash three unruly youngsters as we explored our first foreign soil and she was no doubt glad and relieved to get us back on board.

Two days later we landed at Marseilles, the first seaport of France, and it was the same procedure: a charge down the gangway and off to see what the place offered, while Mum continued to battle to keep control of us – and of the purse strings.

Our wandering ways were bound to get us in trouble and they did – the next day.

That was when we docked at Genoa in Italy and the boys from Carrick Knowe hit the town. Three inquiring minds, three sets of legs wanting to go in different directions, one harassed parent. Time to go back to the ship. By then we were in the middle of Genoa. Where was the harbour? We didn't know. And it was getting close to curfew time.

Tears started, and as a fully fledged twelve-year-old I felt somehow responsible. After all, in his letters Dad had told me in time-honoured fashion that as the oldest son I had to look after everybody else and here we were, a week after sailing, lost in the middle of an Italian city where Carrick Knowe Scottish was not the lingua franca.

We hailed a taxi – that was the second taxi in our lives so we were really living it up. The problem was that with the first taxi in Edinburgh the driver had no difficulty in understanding 'Waverley Station'; '*Dunnottar Castle*' was lost on the Genoa taxi driver.

Then he had the bright idea of driving us to the police station. We thought we were going to be locked up but he was only looking for help – or somebody who could speak English. We were out of luck. I was surprised because I thought all Italians spoke English – but the only ones I had known were back home serving ice cream or fish and chips.

Then the policeman found a bit of inspiration and took us to another room where there was a large map of the city. On the map we saw a dockland area and eagerly pointed it out. Smiles and relief all round and we were soon back on board.

We sailed the next evening, and after midnight Mum woke me in the cabin and whispered to me that I should be on deck with the adults to see a wonderful sight. I tiptoed out without disturbing my sleeping brothers and joined the crowd on deck as we glided slowly and silently past the volcano Stromboli.

We were fifty miles off the southern coast of Italy, and the peak of the Stromboli cone 3,000 feet above the sea was glowing menacingly in the dark (I learned later that it had been known among mariners since ancient times as the 'lighthouse of the Tyrennian').

It was very much in the news at the time and I knew it had something to do with a scandal involving the actress Ingrid Bergman. Twelve-year-old boys in those days knew nothing about scandals but I realised as I gazed with the rapt adults at the glowing Stromboli that this was a significant sighting.

(It was that year, 1950, that Ingrid Bergman married the film director Roberto Rossellini amid what was described as a clamour of public indignation. *The International Film Encyclopaedia* by Ephraim Katz states that the fact that they both left their spouses to enter into their union and lived as lovers before they could get married both scandalised and titillated the public and led to an unofficial boycott in America and other countries of their films. They met while filming *Stromboli*, and the screen outcome is described as a critical and commercial disaster).

So we moved on to our next port of call. Had we learned the lesson of our wandering ways? Perhaps – but the next stop was Port Said, the seaport of Egypt and the northern entrance to the Suez Canal. This was our first taste of Africa, and while Gibraltar, Marseilles and Genoa had a welcoming familiarity about them this was completely different and we felt disinclined to wander around.

It was not threatening. It just seemed to have a sign up which said to us in the Scots vernacular 'gang warily'. So we did not gang at all. Besides, there was enough to see from the ship itself, and the intense heat made the swimming pool even more welcome. I also sought refuge in cards and draughts and, in addition, I had my work to do.

Work? There are frequent references in my diary to 'helping the barman' or 'stewards'. What I was doing, in fact, was clearing away the empty glasses during the day. My salary was a 'tikki' (three-penny) orange, and this gave me a measure of self-importance when I was at that halfway stage of being too old to be one of the children and too young to be allowed among the teenagers.

There were, in fact, quite a few rows about whether or not I should go to the children's tea at 5.30 or live it up at the dinner at 7. I got to that dinner occasionally, but when I started working for the barman, as I saw it, I had definitely left the kids behind.

Then disaster. 'I have been sacked,' the diary laments. Made redundant at twelve. I think I had stretched it a bit by clearing the glasses away in the evening during the dances when couples were clinching in the moonlight. Somebody had complained about a youngster's presence in such steamy circumstances, and my brief sojourn as a worker was over. I was a kid again. But one with disappearing inhibitions.

At Port Said we had a visit from a gully-gully man who produced startled chickens from waistcoat pockets and performed other tricks and magic for our entertainment.

I should add that we had on board our own professional magician, Jasper Maskelyne who, I was told, was quite famous in the world of magic and was a member of a well-known family of magicians. I did note, however, that he and his wife were in Tourist Class so I reckoned he could not have been that hot. Years later I learned how wrong I was – Maskelyne had been employed by the army during the war as a camouflage expert and he was certainly no stranger to the Suez Canal because he had camouflaged it during the war using dozens of mirror-covered cones and he fooled the Germans.

But he was a bitter man because after the war he did not get the recognition he felt he deserved and here he was in 1950 making his way to East Africa. He went on to open a driving school in Nairobi and died of alcoholism, alone and forgotten, at the age of seventy.

But I digress – back to the gully-gully man, who fascinated me. What was he doing on board? Where did he learn all his tricks?

Eight years earlier Evelyn Waugh had wondered the same thing when he encountered a gully-gully man on board the *Rhodesia Castle* at Port Said. He wrote in *A Tourist in Africa*: 'I have often wondered about the history of these performers, more comedians than conjurers who, as far as I know, are peculiar to the [Suez] Canal. The craft, I have been told, is hereditary.'

We sailed from Port Said through the Suez Canal and I was amazed at how close we were to the side of the canal and to the ships going in the opposite direction. Port Sudan was the next stop and this is where I discovered a peculiar fascination for what were called the 'fuzzy wuzzies'. They were the Port Sudan labourers who work on board loading sacks of grain into the bowels of the vessel.

They worked in blistering heat, their bodies glistening in the sun – dirty, smelly and cheerful, singing and chanting as they lifted and stacked. I sat and watched them all afternoon, getting as close to them as possible, quite unafraid, wishing I could speak their language and ask a few questions.

The good-natured smiles we exchanged were language enough. To me, this was what it was all about. We really were in Africa now and the natives were certainly friendly.

Aden was next, with more blistering heat. Mum ventured ashore with one or two other adults, leaving the wanderers behind, but she returned with comics and sweets so we forgave her.

On leaving Aden we hit the first really stormy weather. Flying fish landed on the deck and I held one of them in my hand. My brother Kelman was one of the victims of the storm and became terribly seasick. He told one of the stewards who visited him that he wanted his body to be taken back to Scotland. This quote went right round the ship and so tickled the captain that he paid Kelman a visit in his cabin – Tourist Class and all, and no charge.

On 8 June we arrived at Mombasa in Kenya and we stayed there for four days. It seemed so near yet so far because we were by then in East Africa and eager to see Dad and our new home. I saw a large shark being caught at the edge of the harbour and made sure I got close enough to touch its fin. 'I can hardly believe it – it was a massive maneater,' I noted, making another early use of hyperbole.

We finally reached Dar es Salaam, the haven of peace, on 15 June, a month after we had sailed from Tilbury. This was Africa at its finest, a semicircular landlocked bay with the waves lapping the sandy shore dotted with palm trees – let's have a look at those coconuts – and blue skies that were mirrored in the blue sea.

In those days the arriving vessels at Dar es Salaam had to anchor offshore and the passengers were ferried ashore in smaller vessels. We crowded excitedly at the deck rail looking for the one and only familiar face on the continent and I noticed this speedboat cutting its way through the water in our direction. The man at the helm had a handlebar moustache and that was not Dad.

Minutes later the guy with the moustache was on board embracing Mum, which left me feeling more than a little nonplussed until I realised that it *was* Dad. He'd managed to steer clear, for the most part, of his razor and, get this, he was wearing shorts. I was looking forward to the day when I would be allowed to dispense with shorts and be part of the long trouser brigade and here was Dad turning the clock back.

He was not alone. All the men waiting to meet and greet were in shorts – mostly white shorts and white shirts – and they were barking out orders in Swahili to burly Africans who lifted heavy cases with ease on to their shoulders and heads, muttered something about *Bwana* and headed off. I looked around for Johnny Weissmuller but he was nowhere in sight.

Soon we were on shore and Dad was behind the wheel of a car. 'Welcome to Dar es Salaam, lads,' he said, as he carefully manoeuvred the car past a rickshaw. We just stared at him. After eight months we were almost on the shy side because this was a different Dad – that outfit, that bronzed face, that ginger moustache.

A lizard suddenly landed on the windscreen, hesitated to catch its breath and disappeared. 'That happens all the time,' said Dad with a smile, 'and a lot more than that.'

Our destination was Mgalani Camp on the outskirts of Dar es Salaam. That's where the civil servants and their families stayed until housing was available. The accommodation was thatched roof huts, *bandas* as they were called, but we would have been disappointed had it been anything else.

We did not live in the *banda* alone – there was plenty of entertainment provided by a wide variety of strange visitors. The battle for life and death took place nightly on the walls and ceilings as lizards stalked moths and other insects and frequently lost their balance to clatter down on the table or sideboard then get up unhurt and rush to the hunt again.

We were immediately told that we had to shake out our shoes each morning in case insects were taking shelter there – in particular scorpions, which could be particularly nasty. That was after we had spent the night battling with mosquitoes who found me a tasty morsel on that very first night despite having the supposed benefit of a mosquito net.

The first morning we awoke to the sound of a tinkling teaspoon stirring the sugar in the cup. *'Jambo Bwana,'* was the greeting as the tea was laid on the table while we scratched our mosquito bites, rubbed our eyes and wondered who this benevolent intruder was.

It was Nasoro and he was our houseboy. I couldn't quite grasp this. What was wrong with Mum? Why was this guy making the beds and the breakfast? Get used to it, kid, this is the way of life in Tanganyika. You are in the colonies now. You are a *Bwana Kidogo* (a 'small *Bwana*' but a *bwana* nonetheless).

This was all too good to be true. There had been enough to take in during the four weeks on the ship. But this last twenty-four hours had been overwhelming. The sun was shining. It was another great day.

'Right,' said Dad, 'we'll go and show you Dar es Salaam and maybe spend the afternoon on the beach.'

Great. This was the life. Then he had to go and spoil it.

Looking at me with that moustached grin, he said, 'Then we'll talk about your school.'

Rickshaws, Sharks, Death - and the Ghost Town of Africa

The secondary school for most of the European children in East Africa was the Prince of Wales School in Nairobi, over 750 miles away. It was a boarding school and it was expensive. I knew my parents were aware of this but they were willing to grit their teeth and pay the costs.

There was one snag. The annual intake was in January after you had passed the necessary examination. This was June. I was a keen enough scholar and was looking forward to getting back to school but when we learned that I would have to wait until January before I could go to the Prince of Wales School – assuming I passed the exam – I was able to put aside my zeal for learning and was quite happy to play a waiting game while sampling the novel and exotic delights of Dar es Salaam.

After all, there was so much to see and do. The beaches were fabulous, the weather was superb and I had no doubt that I could put in enough swatting to make sure I passed this exam, whenever and wherever it might be.

But Dad had other ideas. 'You'll just have to go to St Joseph's Convent in the meantime,' he said. This had not been part of my game plan and I certainly was not too keen on the idea. St Joseph's was the Catholic school in Dar es Salaam. We were not Catholics but Dad had obviously been in touch and found that they would be quite happy to take me in for a term or two.

Mercifully, my debut at St Joseph's was postponed, because only three days after arriving in Dar es Salaam I was whipped off to hospital and had my appendix removed. A bit earlier and the operation would have had to be conducted on the high seas.

I felt a bit of a hero and was feted and pampered. In those days having your appendix removed was quite a big operation and a bit of convalescence was involved before you were back to full fitness. But the bubble would soon burst.

It was on 18 June that I had my first day at St Joseph's. I approached it with total apprehension and it was justified. We were taught by nuns, and this was a new experience to me. Most of the pupils were Asian or Goan. I was one of a handful of European kids and my paler-than-most face made it obvious that I was a new arrival. This did not bother me but it was my introduction to racism.

The colour of a person's skin had meant nothing to me. On the *Dunnottar Castle* on the way out, it has to be said, the only non-whites I saw were walking foreign streets or were humping bags of corn on the ship in the heat of Port Said so I had no real close contact with them. To me they were different but interesting and I wanted to meet them and chat to them.

The tables were turned somewhat at the St Joseph's Convent and it was I who was something of a rarity. Most of the white people were able to send their children to posh boarding schools, so why was he here? And doesn't he speak English with a funny accent? I would not say I felt any prejudice or animosity but I know that I was a curiosity and was being treated as such. I was being stared at and laughed at and felt decidedly uncomfortable, even threatened.

In a society which was very much a White Man's society I was on the receiving end of a colour bias.

My diary entries did not mince their words and are as severe a condemnation of a school that you will ever get from a schoolboy who had previously enjoyed school life.

My first day: 'It was pure murder.' Next day: 'I went to school. It is horrible.' Next day: 'I went to the murder house.' 'School is nothing except pure murder.' 'I hate the murder house.' The message pretty soon got through to my parents. I mutinied, said I would not go back to that school and that if I was forced to I wanted to go back home to Scotland.

I can never actually remember being told that I would not have to go back. My diary tells me that there were several days on the trot when I was 'unwell' and was unable to go to school. It was an undoubted con and I suspect my parents were silent fellow conspirators.

So I never went back, and had six school-less months to enjoy

Dar es Salaam, mindful of the fact that at the end of November I was going to have to sit examinations which might or might not take me on that great journey to the Prince of Wales School in Nairobi.

Dar es Salaam had plenty to offer a twelve-year-old with an inquiring mind and a streak of independence that was not born out of overconfidence but of a determination to do one's own thing. There was not a rebel lurking in me, far from it – more of a non-conforming individualist who could also be a pretty good team player.

I'd had my doubts about going to East Africa in the first place but that was probably because I thought Scotland was the only place in the world where they played football. Now that I had arrived in Dar es Salaam and had been overwhelmed by it all I was ready for what Africa had to offer me, and over the years Africa was to prove to be bounteous.

Dar es Salaam (Haven of Peace in Arabic) was the capital of Tanganyika Territory. Tanganyika's conquerors in centuries past had been Arab and Portuguese and the great explorers such as Livingstone, Stanley, Thomson and Speke had crossed its jungles.

Dar had been built by Majid, the Sultan of Zanzibar, during his reign, which lasted from 1856 until 1870. Zanzibar was then at the hub of the slave trade so it could be said that what is the main town of what is now Tanzania – after the merger of Tanganyika and Zanzibar – is a legacy of the profits of this evil trade. Dar had become an important Arab city ruled in turn by the sultans of Muscat and Zanzibar but it later declined into a small fishing village.

It was the Germans who changed all that. Dar's fortunes were restored by the Germans who ruled from 1886 until 1918. Bagamoyo was the headquarters of German East Africa between 1886 and 1891 when the Germans made Dar es Salaam, forty-four miles to the south, the capital. Bagamoyo, founded at the end of the eighteenth century, had been the starting point for Stanley's journey to find Livingstone – the starting point, in fact, of many famous and little-known journeys into the interior.

It was the trading port for the ivory and slave trade. Once they reached Bagamoyo the slaves and ivory were shipped by dhow to

Zanzibar then dispatched all over the world. Today, Bagamoyo is a centre for dhow sailboat building and the Bagamoyo College of Arts has an international reputation.

Tanganyika had been part of the scramble for Africa by the Great Powers in the last century and most of it by 1886 had ended up as German East Africa. It was conquered by South African and British troops in 1918 and since 1920 had been administered by Britain under mandate.

The German influence was still very much evident in Dar – the buildings on the seafront, particularly the three-storeyed old colonial Post Office, were very Germanic. The central hotel and one of the main watering holes for the British, the New Africa Hotel, had started life as the Kaiserhoff. Some German words had been adopted into Swahili and I spoke to many Africans who could remember living under German rule.

Dar was a cosmopolitan community which was very much compartmentalised along the lines of nationality and/or occupation. There was, for example, the Hellenic Club and the Goan Club and, inevitably, the Caledonian Society, and nobody complained about them being racist or discriminatory. Then there was the Gymkhana Club – that, of course, was for Europeans only – and if you worked on the railways there was the Railway Club. The British Legion Club was another favourite.

Dad worked for the East African Posts and Telegraphs; he was engineering while others were postal. For some reason the engineering guys thought they were superior to postal although they got on well socially.

But I was watching and learning. I had a mental tag for all those who came over the door – and there were many, because Dar was a very social place – or for those who were spotted in one of the clubs or at the social Mecca for the Dar Set, the Ocean Breeze.

That tag said simply 'he's Postal', 'he's Engineering', 'he's Railways', 'he's Commercial'. The prize tag was 'he's a £1,000-a-year man'. I knew that if that was what you earned you were top dog and those bringing in that sort of money were spoken of in hushed tones.

There was another category – the groundnut scheme people.

Early in 1947 the Labour Government had launched a scheme to make Tanganyika a major peanut producing country, providing margarine for the undernourished people of Great Britain. It seemed a good idea at the time in the post-war euphoria and determination to do something different but it was a disastrous and costly failure and was finally abandoned around the time that we arrived in Dar. Around £36 million – a lot of money in the cash-hungry Britain of 1947 – had been poured into the African soil without producing a single peanut.

Many of the British civil servants who had worked on that scheme moved to new jobs in Dar. It was not their fault that they had been associated with what was generally accepted as a major Government cock-up but they became tagged as 'ex-groundnut scheme' people or 'the groundnut drop-outs' and that bore something of a stigma.

The groundnut scheme had been born and died in Kongwa after a brief lifetime and it was a place I never managed to visit. I was curious about it, having heard tales of the great initial high hopes and grand living in the bush of Kongwa.

That grand living saw Kongwa's main street becoming known as Millionaire's Row, where high officials lived when they were not flying off to Dar or London. They had it made, so it was reckoned, but if ever there was an African bubble waiting to burst this was it. A year after the British Government launched the scheme it built a school in Kongwa which was set up as the European boarding school for Tanganyika – mainly for the offspring of the Europeans working on the scheme. Alumni do not exist. It was not long before the groundnut scheme, the ornate bungalows and the school were confined to the dust of history because the scheme has been rightfully dubbed as one of the most dramatic failures of late British colonial development. One friend of my father's who had worked in Kongwa paid the town a visit soon after the collapse and was saddened to see that the roads in the town were breaking up, the railway signs removed, the airstrip overgrown and 'for sale' signs everywhere.

At one time Kongwa had housed some 2,000 men and women from Britain and 30,000 locals. It was said that half the liquor imported into Tanganyika was consumed in Kongwa. Prostitutes, thieves and drunks abounded. It was like the Wild West in the middle of the jungle. It became the first ghost town in Africa made by the white man.

The story of Kongwa, the high life and the low life, was known to us all, so carrying the label of a 'groundnut drop-out' gave somebody a bit of unwelcome distinction.

On 23 July 1950 we finally vacated Mgalani Camp and moved out of the town to the new development at Oyster Bay and to our new house furnished in the sparse Government fashion but like a mansion to the brothers Dow. 'What a smashing house we have,' boasts the diary.

The gardens had been virtually hacked out of the bush and ours looked more like a sisal plantation than anything else but at last we were free from the restricted space of Mgalani and had a place of our own.

On that first day at Oyster Bay the three of us were taken into the garden for a photograph that was to go back home to let them all see that we had finally made it to the real Africa.

We wore khaki shorts and straw hats, no shirts. Irvin clutched two bananas (still a rarity in Britain at that time), Kelman had a lovely bunch of coconuts and I had a pawpaw in one hand and a pineapple in the other. We looked decidedly uncomfortable and self-conscious amid the sisal and scrub but it was definitely one for the family album.

We had to learn to adjust quickly to the domestic life of Dar.

Drinking water, for a start, was precious. You dare not drink water straight from the tap – it had to be boiled first of all. Then you had to wait patiently until it was cool enough to be poured into bottles. The bottles were then put into the fridge to cool off and chill – then you could consume. Gulp is a better word, because we were always thirsty. Woe betide any member of the family who sneaked through to the kitchen and started on one of the bottles while the water was still only lukewarm.

In that kitchen you had to learn to live with the ants, who were the scavengers and housekeepers. The legs of the tables and the fridge had to stand in tin cans filled with water or oil so that the ants could not climb up but everything else was fair game for the ants and they missed nothing.

A piece of meat or a grain of sugar on the floor or a dead insect – always plenty of them around – became the ants' booty. Go into the kitchen most nights, switch on the light and you will invariably see a long trail of ants progressing up the wall carrying their tasty prize into a crack where the wall meets the ceiling.

If you were in a mischievous mood you would use a long brush to knock to the floor whatever the ants were carrying. The confused ants would scurry around gently touching heads as if conversing and they were undoubtedly saying to each other, 'What the hell happened there?' But they would soon regroup and return to the floor to find the booty and start all over again. You never took their hoard away a second time because you soon built up a certain amount of admiration and respect for them.

While sitting in the lounge at night you had to beware of the buzz bombers. They were large, ponderous beetles which rose slowly as their wings struggled with the heavy body. They were easy targets for a swipe with a book or a newspaper; if you left them they would slowly gain close to ceiling height then suddenly stop and crash downwards. They always seemed to land in your glass or cup and if you stood on them or hit them too hard with the book they gave off a strong smell. No wonder they were also known as shite beetles.

Most of the spare time was spent swimming and the swimming club was the focal point. It was not so much a club – more of a wooden hut, but offshore was a raft supported by empty barrels. It had a diving board and a high dive and it was the place to be. Depending on the tide and the current it could be an easy swim out or it could be a bit of a struggle. Some did not bother with the struggle, preferring the safety of the beach; I always made it – that independent streak again – and always insisted that my younger brothers do the same for the sake of the family honour.

The raft was at the edge of a strait which took ships into Dar harbour. At the other side was the wreck of a German ship from the First World War. We never had the courage to swim the full width of the strait to inspect the wreck but we did venture fairly far out and waved to the passengers on the liners as they moved in or out of the harbour.

That was on the foolhardy side. We had been told that sharks followed the ships so far up the strait but not into the confined harbour – one of the finest natural harbours in the world. They lingered in the channel waiting for another ship to come out and followed it. The reason was that feeding was made a lot easier for them with the kitchen waste that was dumped overboard. Feeding would have been even easier still had they moved in on the swimming club and picked up some of the two-legged morsels flapping about in a show of bravado.

An unusual form of transport in our early Dar days were rickshaws. They are said to have been invented in Japan by an American Baptist missionary in 1871. Somehow they found their way to Dar and I was determined to try one out. It was a memorable experience but not one I was anxious to repeat.

Rickshaws were not expensive except to twelve-year-olds with not a lot of change in their pockets, but one day I found the cash – and the courage – to take a rickshaw from the swimming club into the centre of Dar, a journey of about two miles. I was quite embarrassed by it all, sitting there lording it through the streets while a human horse puffed and panted to pull me to my destination.

It struck me as pretty demeaning and I was not surprised or disappointed when the local authority soon afterwards banned them from the streets of Dar. That, of course, meant that the human horses became unemployed – but I suppose that for quite a few the Olympic Games beckoned!

In Dar death meant a swift departure from the scene. I remember the tragic death of one of Dad's engineering colleagues. He was only thirty-four, with a young wife and son – he died suddenly one morning and the funeral was at 4 o'clock in the afternoon. That's how it was in Dar – it was a very hot climate and in pre-fridge days the dead had to be disposed of pretty quickly. I have often wondered if this is not perhaps a good idea anyway – better than waiting days for the funeral. The grief-stricken get it all over in the one day.

Every family needed a car and a new one was the symbol of having made it. It was all the men ever seemed to talk about –

their car and which one they would buy when they had completed their first tour of duty and would go home to the UK for leave.

People on their second tour could usually afford a new car and I dreamed of the day when we would get our new car. I knew every make of car in Dar and could recognise it immediately from afar. I can always remember the one that impressed me most was a Standard Vanguard. There were not many in Dar and I actually got a lift in one once. My enjoyment of the occasion was somewhat stultified by the fact that the driver had only one arm. The gear change was on the steering column and changing gear was quite a skilful manoeuvre.

Dad had three of us to educate at boarding school so he was nowhere near getting the new car that was the subject of our dreams. In fact, he went to the other extreme and found what must have been the oldest car in Tanganyika. It was called a Ford Eiffel and, according to Dad, only a few had been made by the Germans before the war. When I saw it, I was not sure which war he was talking about. (In fact, it was special made by the German Government around 1938 to commemorate Henry Ford's seventy-fifth anniversary).

It was dark green with the remnants of a canvas top. The only window was in the front, so when it rained and the wind was in the wrong direction you got a soaking. The windscreen wiper operated with great reluctance and with nothing that resembled efficiency.

The springs in the back seat punctured your posterior with painful persistence. The car continually jumped out of top gear so that Dad had to keep his left hand on the gear lever and steer with his right. The horn was two bare wires which dangled down from the steering column and had to be earthed to the column to make a rasping noise.

Trying to steer, stay in top gear and use the horn at the same time with a windscreen wiper that was on a constant go-slow was challenging, to say the least. The steering wheel itself was a bit dodgy – one night it came off in Dad's hand as he negotiated the tricky bend before Selander Bridge on the way back to Oyster Bay from the cinema.

Dad had a penchant for giving things a name and the car was christened Bessie. Had they had MOT certification in those days she would have been put down instantly. As it was, Bessie chugged away for a few more years, providing us with many a laugh and heartache and almost becoming a member of the family as well as the family trademark recognised throughout Dar.

She made us look like the Beverley McHillbillies. When Dad eventually sold her, the new owner took off the wheels, put a few thick sticks from window to window and dear old Bessie became a hen house.

But Bessie was kept in a garage bigger than my bedroom. There was no door on it and at the front hung a swing which Dad had installed for us. Where did he get that thick rope that was hooked on to the large beam above the garage entrance? It so happened that he knew the hangman at Dar prison and he was renewing his accoutrements so Dad got the old rope for the swing and we had many pleasant swinging hours with a rope which had sent quite a few men to their maker. When Dad came home at night it was our task to get out and hold the swing back so that Bessie could get into the garage.

I remember one particular night when there was the usual whine and squeak from Bessie as she left the main tarmacked road and zimmered and bounced into the stony track that cut through the sisal and took one final right hand turn before arriving at our house.

In my usual leisurely fashion I got up and ambled outside towards the garage to grab the hangman's rope and pull the swing aside so that Bessie could get in. This clear, moonlit night, as usual, I was followed by the two dogs, Laddie and Tim, and by the time Dad had turned the first corner I could hear Bessie going at what, for her, was quite a pace. And the horn was rasping.

I could picture Dad speeding along with one hand on the steering wheel and the other frantically holding the bare wires to the steering column to emit this moan from the vehicle. In the bright moonlight I soon saw the real thing and it was just as I had briefly pictured it apart from one difference. The look on Dad's face was one of panic.

OK Dad, I thought, I've seen you – I'm on my way to the

swing and will get there before you. I could not understand what all the fuss was about – I had never let him down. He swung Bessie into the driveway and got her into the garage at a speed which would have been an achievement for a young 'un. For Bessie, this was Grand Prix stuff. Dad leapt out of the car and shouted: 'Get into the house quick – there's a leopard out there.'

He had caught it in the full glare of the headlights as he turned off the main road and he had seen it running after him. Given that it was a slow-moving car with no windows Dad did not feel fully protected and he knew that I would be meeting him with the dogs.

Dogs were a bit of a delicacy for leopards and we'd heard that one or two of them had disappeared in the area over the last few nights after a leopard had been seen in the vicinity. To us, that was just a rumour – but the look in Dad's eyes and the speed with which the two of us got into the house along with the two dogs confirmed that the rumour had four legs and spots.

By then we had more than just two dogs. We had acquired a dozen chickens, six ducks, about ten pigeons and a monkey. The monkey spent a lot of time chained up in a kennel but occasion-ally escaped and romped over the roof of the house before deciding or being persuaded to return to base. He used to perch on Kelman's shoulder when he was on his bike and they were great pals. One horrible afternoon a roaming Alsatian got to him as he was chained and trapped and tore him to pieces.

Snakes were also quite a hazard. The monkey, the dogs and the chickens were all bitten by various snakes – though amazingly the attacks were fatal for only one or two chickens – so you had to be constantly on your guard. I killed one which had got into the henhouse but this was a python and not life-threatening and I had the upper hand with a big axe.

The other one I dispatched was a nastier customer. It came at me from ground level from the monkey's house – the monkey was on the roof at the time and we can guess why. I stood waiting with legs apart and a big boulder held aloft waiting for the perfect moment to strike. The snake made a beeline for me, eyes firmly fixed on mine, and when it was a couple of feet away I dropped the stone with devastating affect. The general consensus was that it was a black mamba and certainly something very dangerous. It mattered not – my brothers were determined to allocate me hero status and I was not going to argue.

But this idyllic life spiced with danger had to end sometime. I was, after all, still only a schoolboy with a lot of education ahead of me and I would soon have to sit the Kenya Preliminary Examination in the hope of gaining entry to the Prince of Wales School. This is when those supposed long hours of swatting would pay off.

Swatting? The only swatting I had really done was in collaboration with Dad. All civil servants had to pass Swahili examinations as part of their career progression and many nights a week I used to take Dad through the language course in preparation for his exam. This was no chore – I enjoyed learning and speaking Swahili and was only too keen to be as proficient as possible. This might have helped Dad in his upcoming exam but it was not one of the subjects on my exam schedule so it did not help me, although it was to prove a big plus later when my school days were behind me.

Apart from that I'd studied swimming and more swimming. I'd dived deep and swum long, supposedly where the sharks lay in waiting.

I'd swatted up on the Portuguese man-of-war and how to avoid his painful sting in the Indian Ocean. I'd made a special study of the Dar es Salaam society and had a pretty good knowledge of the £1,000-a-year guys.

I could tell when a hen was going to lay or go broody. I'd learned how to tangle with a snake and catch a monkey on the roof of the house. This was hardly the best preparation for an exam which would shape my future.

This was 30 October 1950. The last time I had been at school, apart from those desperate mercifully few days at St Joseph's, was in Edinburgh on 6 May. My first exam was the next day. I had to do something. I did – I spent the day at the swimming club.

The next day Dad drove me to a house in another part of Oyster Bay and I was introduced to Mrs Roper. She was going to supervise me when I took the exam. She bade me a polite 'good morning' and so did the parrot in the cage in the kitchen.

I was ushered through to the lounge and told to sit down at a table. She produced an arithmetic examination paper, told me I had an hour, and she withdrew with a smile. I stared at the piece of paper in front of me and struggled frantically to get the brain going again – my luck to have to start with arithmetic, not my best subject – and it was a long and tortured hour. The next paper was English and I was much more comfortable with that.

When finished I arose from the table and she offered me a soft drink while I waited for Dad to come and collect me. On balance, I felt quite pleased with myself. This was not really as bad as I had expected and I reckoned that I had probably passed. Then Mrs Roper spoiled it all by saying, 'We'll see you again tomorrow.'

So I was back again tomorrow to face Arithmetic, Part Two. Sitting in Mrs Roper's lounge on a hot tropical afternoon in a compact little house surrounded by palm trees with a conver- sational parrot in the kitchen and the crickets chirruping away outside was unreal. I had to fight hard to concentrate and take it all seriously, to grapple with the fact that this cosy, laid back examination process was me at the crossroads. If I took the wrong step, hell's teeth, it could be a year at St Joseph's Convent before I was allowed to try again.

I was certainly paying dearly for all those hours of sea, sun and sand. Somehow, I got through Arithmetic, Part Two. Then there was English, Part Two, which did not really worry me, and I was back in the afternoon for geography.

The next day was the final paper – history. That afternoon it was back to the swimming pool, wondering if I would ever become a real schoolboy again.

Well, I did, although I was soon to learn that life at the Prince of Wales School was far from what I imagined would be the life of a real schoolboy. I passed my exams, not exactly with flying colours because I was told I would be in 1C – 1A was the cream of the first year. That did not surprise or concern me (I soon climbed out of it) – the main thing was that I had got through.

First of all, I had to be kitted out. Dad must have groaned when he saw the clothes list the headmaster had sent – shirts, shorts, stockings, shoes, blazer and my first pair of long trousers.

They all had to be made to measure at the Asian tailors and getting the shoes made to measure was an interesting experience – the shoemaker opened a large book, pointed to a blank page and invited me to step on it with my bare foot. With a pencil he carefully drew around the foot then measured it and that was that – come back next week and the shoes will be here.

But school was not until the start of the following year. I still had a bit of swimming to do. Christmas was different – 90 degrees in the shade and more swimming. But even I had to admit that I was getting weary. School could not come too quickly. All my clothes had been bought and labelled as per the school instructions.

And the instructions were pretty explicit. The 1951 edition of the school's 'Notes for the Guidance of Parents and New Boys' states:

> All garments, rugs, shoes, brushes etc. must be clearly marked with the name and initials of the boy in some obvious place. They will be inspected on arrival and the owner of unmarked garments will be fined (initials only won't do). Each boy must bring an accurate list with him. We do our best to prevent losses at the *dhobi* and elsewhere. Sheer carelessness and inefficient marking are responsible for most of the losses that do occur.

So it was seldom the school's fault and with a warning like that everything I took with me was clearly marked. If Mum had been able to get away with it I am sure she would have tattooed my name on my forehead.

The notes contained other warnings such as, 'Please be very careful to see that the boy brings with him medical record sheets and health certificates. A boy who fails to bring his health certificate may be isolated in the sanitarium until it arrives.'

I would not say that the school was by now beginning to lose some of its allure but I got the distinct impression that if you stepped out of line you were in trouble. There was more. We were also told that we had to bring a mosquito net because the Medical Department 'considers that in exceptional circumstances epidemic malaria might occur. It would then be possible for me (the Headmaster) to order every boy to sleep under a net should an emergency arise'.

It was beginning to sound like a real barrel of fun. But I was not to be put off. Beside, the final paragraph of the notes contained what the Headmaster no doubt regarded as a wee bit of a reassurance for parents who had had the courage to read that far: 'The above notes are full of "do" and "don't". My intention is to save us from spending unnecessary time putting right minor muddles that need never occur so that we have the time and energy to attend to our proper business, which is to teach your son and look after him generally.'

It seemed as though I was being groomed for the French Foreign Legion but my bags were packed and I was ready for the off on the Monday night, 15 January 1951. I was catching the train from Dar es Salaam and Nairobi was my destination.

Apart from my parents and my brothers, I did not know a soul on the platform that night. Kids of all ages and nationalities were getting ready to board that train, many of them with that confident look that said, 'I've done this before.'

I honestly did not know what lay ahead. I did not know how long it would take me to get to Nairobi (I assumed it was the next morning) but I knew that I had a fair bit of East Africa to cover before I got there.

The farewells were said and I boarded the train, and soon the Dar es Salaam platform was a dim light as we moved into the darkness of Africa. I was not holding back any tears – I was looking forward to it all, eagerly anticipating the fun and the adventure.

Nairobi tomorrow? I wondered. Just think, said the mind, tomorrow at this time you will be in a school dormitory among lots of new friends.

Little did I know. Nairobi was more than four days and three nights away. I was a wet-behind-the-ears boarder and that meant I was classed as 'rabble'. At boarding school they took no prisoners. The prefects had the power to cane you on the backside and draw blood, which they frequently did.

Sorry, Jim, but this was no joy ride to a pleasure park. Think back to those long days on the beach. You were heading for a different Africa.

The Rabble with a Crew Cut

My diary for Monday, 15 January 1951, says matter-of-factly, 'At night I left for Nairobi (Prince of W) by train. Yippee, at last.'

I slept quite well on the slow, shuddering steam train as it wound its way inland from the coast and this was despite the fact that I had plenty of mosquitoes to keep me company. In the morning we arrived at Morogoro and I just followed the crowd as we disembarked and headed for the breakfast hotel in the centre of the small town at the base of the Uluguru Mountains.

I was not clutching an itinerary or timetable which set it all out for me. Like the other rookies, I just followed the senior boys who had done it all before and appeared to know their way around. Keep close to them and we will get to school some day. While they looked on us as newcomers with a certain amount of disdain and misplaced superiority because, well, we were newcomers, I cannot recall anything other than help and cooperation on the journeys to school.

In fact, we all approached it with an amazing amount of naivety; I was regarded as one of the more experienced of the newcomers in that I had been in Africa long enough to get my knees brown, but I'd hardly been beyond the beach at Dar es Salaam and this trans-Africa safari was every bit as new to me as it was to the other tyros on the trip.

Many of them looked as though they had just stepped off the ship or plane from England on their first adventure away from home, and here they were, wide-eyed and whiter than white, trekking across Africa, blindly putting their trust in strangers.

The destination that first morning was the Acropole Hotel, where we bought ourselves breakfast. We were already building up a cocky confidence. It was certainly the first meal I had ever bought myself and it does give you a feeling of power. Unfortunately, that power was running out already because funds were getting low.

I suppose Dad thought that all would be found for us on the trip to school and that the pocket money he gave me for the journey, five shillings, was just for the odd little frivolity and emergency. In fact, we had to pay for all our meals and we were hungry and thirsty travellers.

I did have other money on me: this was the tuck shop money for the entire term and I was to hand it to my housemaster as soon as I got to school. I was warned by Dad in no uncertain terms that I would be in big trouble if that envelope did not reach the housemaster intact.

I learned that the next leg of our journey was by bus to Korogwe, which is in the heart of the sisal country. My diary laments that I left my hat in the Morogoro hotel – Dad was so pleased that he had been able to kit me out fully according to the list supplied by the school and I was an important item short already.

Most of the road to Korogwe was just a wide track through the jungle – it had been built by the German army at the start of the First World War when it was German East Africa. It was hot and humid and bumpy. We did 176 miles, taking about eight hours, and we had what I suppose you would call a health stop. This was to allow Government employees to come on board and spray DDT all over the place. We got used to sitting there with our eyes and mouths shut then waiting for the smell to go. The reason? To kill off any tsetse flies which might have boarded the bus. I don't know that this meant we had passed through tsetse fly territory but any in the bus that survived the onslaught must have been as tough as the chicken we were later to encounter.

We had a couple of stops – the halfway break was at a place called Mziha, where we had lunch and we did our best to slake our thirst.

We always looked forward to the lunch but that was because we were hungry and not because of any culinary skills or fare that were on evidence in the middle of nowhere. The menu and the quality never changed – it was always chicken, and I think the chicken had surrendered.

It has been said of the East African chicken that it is tough, stringy and hard to beat. They have a hardy upbringing, pecking out a dusty and precarious existence on *shambas* which do not offer much so they do not give much back. It has been said that the way to cook a Tanganyika chicken is to boil it in a pot with a stone – and when the stone is soft the chicken is done!

Nonetheless, we felt fortified by this mighty chicken and were ready for the next stop, Handeni, which had been the scene of some skirmishes between the British and the Germans in the First World War and there is a small cemetery there containing some of the British fallen. It was always hot and dusty there and we were always thirsty and hungry. Handeni was the spot where we used to buy sugar cane and munch our way through it during the last quarter of the journey. The price we paid was the runs at night.

By the time we reached Korogwe we were a dust-covered, shattered, dispirited bunch looking for a toilet. I had an added problem: I had no funds. Apart from that envelope, of course, but I was not about to incur Dad's eventual wrath by breaking that open.

There was only one answer: phone home. The problem was that I did not have enough money even for the phone and in those days I knew nothing about reversing charges. But, if nothing else, I was resourceful. I went to the local telephone exchange and told the African in charge that I had to telephone my father in Dar es Salaam.

I told him that I did not have any money but my Dad worked for the telephone company. Please can you put a free call through to him? He must have taken pity on me because it was against all rules and regulations but he was good enough to put me through, and with tears welling, I told Dad of my plight. Yes, of course, open the envelope – you didn't have to phone but it's great to hear from you. How are you getting on? Are you not there yet? What do you mean – you don't get there until Thursday?

Korogwe, a couple of years later, became the venue for a famous football match. On the way back from school, as usual we had time to kill in Korogwe before we took the bus to Morogoro. We saw a group of Africans playing football and we suggested a challenge match. Eight of us took on eight of them and very soon quite a crowd gathered.

We were fit young bucks and were soon starting to run them ragged. After twenty minutes we were five goals up. After an hour we were losing 10–6. We were not as fit as we thought. I started to notice that I could no longer leave the fullback in my dust – he was starting to catch up easily. And their wingers were leaving us panting for breath.

After ninety minutes and several goals against us later we staggered off. I suddenly recognised a face in the crowd. It was the guy who had started the game at fullback – here he was smiling and refreshed as a spectator on the touchline. Other teammates were having the same experience. Then it dawned on us – when a player had had enough he sneaked off and was replaced. We never caught on, but we reckoned we had played twenty of them that afternoon.

But I digress. After that frantic phone call I had made to Dad while having a cash flow problem at Korogwe Dad had reacted to my SOS and after the overnight journey on the train we arrived at Moshi and I was met by Ernie Gresham. He was 'telephone engineering' so he was OK and Dad had asked him to look out for me. I had an evening meal at his house along with his wife, Betty, and this homely touch was just what I needed because, tough guy though I felt I was, I was still a wee chap far away from home in a strange land with a mixed bunch of kids I barely knew.

Moshi was to become my favourite stop on those many journeys to the Prince of Wales School. *Moshi* means smoke in Swahili, and we believed the town had been given that name because it had been a busy railway station. In fact, as I learned later, the explorer Joseph Thomson had visited the Kingdom of Moshi in 1883 while on his troubled trip into Masailand, so the name was there long before the railway line. The smoke that was *moshi* is more likely to have been the moving mist that often scarfed the summit of Africa's highest mountain, Mount Kilimanjaro.

Moshi – it was the German HQ at the start of the First World War and the British took it in 1916 – nestles at the foot of the majestic, snow-capped Kilimanjaro. I thought I had left all the snow behind in Scotland yet here it was in the middle of Africa and I found that hard to believe.

I was not the first one to grapple with incredulity when it came to Kilimanjaro. A German missionary, Johann Rebmann, in May 1848 had been the first European to see Mount Kilimanjaro. He learned that Kilimanjaro was Swahili for 'mountain of Greatness' although the local Wachagga tribe called it the 'Mountain of Whiteness', which is much more descriptive.

Whatever they called it the geographical establishment back home in Europe were not convinced and did not at first believe that so much snow – any at all, in fact – could be found so close to the equator. To this day there is a glacier on the mountain named after Rebmann and it should have in brackets: 'I told you so.'

The snow was still there to greet me and remind me of home just over 100 years later – I was well behind Johann Rebmann but I was a year ahead of Gregory Peck, who lay wounded on the slopes of that majestic mountain and thought of the time he had spent with Ava Gardner and Susan Hayward in the film of the Hemingway novel *The Snows of Kilimanjaro*. (I should be so lucky!)

My Kilimanjaro starring role was in an outdoor swimming pool which was at the base of the mountain and was filled with water from the melted snows of Kilimanjaro. And it was freezing. This was too much of a test for most of my companions, many of them born and bred in East Africa, but when you have swum in the North Sea at Dunbar on the East coast of Scotland you have no problems with a dip at Moshi.

The final leg of the school journey was by train from Moshi to Nairobi, and on the way there we stopped for lunch at Voi, which was where the line from Moshi joined the line from Mombasa. I knew all about Voi, having been an avid reader of the classic *Man-eaters of Tsavo* by Lt Col J H Patterson.

When the builders of the railway line reached Voi from Mombasa in December 1897 man-eating lions seemed to be everywhere, hungry and audacious. One description is that they 'infested' the area, and in 1899 near Voi one particularly bold lion made a night raid on a tent occupied by a road engineer named O'Hara and his family. The hungry lion killed O'Hara while his wife and two children slept beside him.

The book by Patterson, first published in 1907, is the story of the building of a section of the railway from Mombasa to the interior of Uganda. The maneaters were two lions who picked off railway workers – at least twenty-eight of them – at Tsavo, not far from Voi, over a period of nine months and succeeded in stopping work on the line for three weeks. Colonel Patterson hunted them both down and shot them.

Passing through Voi and over the Tsavo Bridge that had been completed only after the maneaters had been disposed of only fifty-three years earlier was a thrill for me – nobody seemed impressed but for them it was either old hat or they had not been lucky enough to have read Colonel Patterson's gripping account of his hunt for the maneaters.

On the return trips from Nairobi to Dar the timetable was different and we had dinner at Voi station at a long table with starched tablecloths in the semi-darkness offered by swinging oil lamps. One roar from outside and I would have been swinging from one of those lamps.

This final stretch from Moshi took us across the Tanganyika border and into Kenya – the excitement was starting to build up among the rookies, and I was no exception. During all those months in Dar es Salaam getting to Nairobi had been the big ambition – once I had passed the exams it loomed closer and I really felt I was going places. This was, after all, the biggest city in East Africa and that's where the train was heading.

Not at any great speed, I hasten to add. Nairobi is 6,000 feet above sea level so it is quite a climb. The train struggled at times up the gradient and we used to get off and walk alongside, full of bravado. Sometimes we would walk behind then run like hell to loud cheers to get on board again. Had the gradient eased or had we tripped and the train shown a sudden burst of speed we would have been left behind in the middle of Africa.

We arrived in Nairobi at ten in the morning that Thursday to be met by the Prince of Wales school bus. The school had been founded in 1931 for the sons of white settlers and administrators and it was run along the lines of British public schools, the good and bad of which I would soon find out.

The bus slowly left the railway station and made its way to the outskirts of Nairobi. The newcomers in our group sat with noses pressed against the dust-covered windows as we waited to see what could be our second home over the next few years.

I was not disappointed – the bus stopped at a magnificent, imposing structure – tall pillars, the school clock, the quadrangle, the white buildings, the flagpole. I'd been smitten by the public school concept after reading so many boys' adventure books set in public schools and here I was arriving at my own boarding school.

The bus drew up near the school quadrangle. I got off slowly and looked at the vast building and wondered where my dormitory was.

I soon came down to earth. I was a newcomer, remember? That meant in Prince of Wales parlance that I was a rabble. Translation: I had no privileges. I was in Junior House and that was well away from the main part of the school. And it was made of wood, one long dormitory with beds on either side. Take off your shoes before you enter the dorm, find your bed, unpack and get on with it.

That first night the last few words I entered in my diary were: 'I've lost my fountain pen.' I was doing well – the hat on the Tuesday and the pen on the Thursday.

I soon learned that I had to come to terms with a new social order. Outside the school it was all basically straightforward – the Europeans were the rulers, the Asian were somewhere in the middle and the Africans worked for us. I did not feel too comfortable with that but accepted that this was the way of East African life. I was very much a conformist and it did not occur to me then that this should be challenged.

Inside the school as a rabble in Junior House I was the lowest form of life. Above me were guys in Intermediate. Above them were the older boys in the school's houses, with names of heroes no doubt expected to act as our inspiration – Clive (of India fame), Scott (of the Antarctic, and not, as I was sorry to discover, Sir Walter), Rhodes (Cecil, inevitably), Hawke (Admiral Edward Hawke, scourge of the French fleet and Lord of the Admiralty 1766–1771), Grigg (Sir Edward, the Governor and Commander-in-Chief of Kenya 1925–1930 who laid the foundation stone for the school in September 1929) and Nicholson, named after the school's first headmaster, a Royal Navy captain who was said to have achieved the 'distinction' of being torpedoed in both wars. Sounded to me like a man not to stand next to on the bridge.

Sitting in higher echelon in the houses were the house prefects. Their top man was the Head of House and that put him among the elite of the School Prefects. The most senior school prefect was the Head of School, the ultimate.

So I was away down the pecking order. There was, however, one caste lower than me – day boys. They did not board. They went home at night to stay with their mummies and daddies while we had to rough it with the rigours of boarding school life. They were known as 'stinkers'.

One stinker for a short spell, I can reveal, was Sir David Steel. He was also a *pongo*, which is a derogatory name for a still-wet-behind-the-ears arrival from Britain, and with his puny, white legs, swatty disposition and dark brown shorts which were too long he was a definite *pongo*. A pongo stinker – a helluvah start to life, but it was obviously good grounding for a splendid Parliamentary career.

Within that hierarchy, there was another major division, nothing to do with race but with nationality. Without doubt, the dominant nationality were the Afrikaaners. I was the only Scot that I could find – I did meet one or two later – and there was a sprinkling of Italians, Germans, Greeks and, just as foreign to me in those days, English, plus one or two Belgians, but it was the Afrikaaners who held sway.

Not only did they outnumber everybody else – they also had their own language and had no hesitation in speaking to each other in Afrikaans when you were in their company. Many did not like that, especially the English, but the English themselves were divided into two camps – the sons of Kenya settlers who originated from England but in the strictest terms were white Kenyans, and the sons of English people who were working on contract in East Africa and would eventually go home (I was a Scottish version).

It was into that maelstrom of pre-puberty and adolescent masculinity that I was plunged, and you either skulked around in the background and saw out your years in what you regarded as safe anonymity or you got stuck in there and showed that you were not just part of the crowd.

I reckon I had four weapons.

First, I was Scottish, and, despite the fact that Scottish explorers had been stretching their legs and spreading their accent across Africa for some time, at the Prince of Wales School in Nairobi in 1951 I was the explorer, the Scottish stranger in their midst. A curiosity is perhaps taking it a bit too far but it made me that bit different – especially when I was soon inevitably nick-named 'Haggis'.

Second, I had a sense of humour. I preferred to laugh or make someone laugh than to shout or cry.

Third, I could show them a thing or two on the sports field. I soon made the football first team and eventually got my school colours. I also proved to be pretty good at the other games, some of which I was learning for the first time, such as hockey and rugby. Ability on the sports field helped immensely to keep you comfortably placed in your relationships with the hierarchy and the dominant groups.

And, fourth, I could be a team player. That is another way of saying that I was able to recognise and pay respect to authority. I did not try to buck the system. Coward? Sure, there was a lot of authority above me and this was a big boarding school where you had to struggle for some sort of place. So I was willing enough to be assertive when I had to but I realised that it was better to toe the line. I knew that each term would bring more seniority and there would be less and less line to toe.

But in the meantime I had to live with the fact that being a rabble was bad enough; being a rebel rabble would be inviting disaster.

Not that I did not occasionally transgress. There were so many rules that you could not help break some of them. You were not allowed, for example (unless you were a teacher or a School Prefect) to take a short cut across the grassed quadrangle. It was a tempting short cut, especially if you were late. And you did not dare wear your shoes on the highly polished floors of the dormitories – unless you were a prefect or above.

The punishment for most offences: the cuts. That is, getting caned on the backside by a prefect. Depending on the severity of the offence you got two, three or four strokes; six was always there as the ultimate thereat but I cannot recall anybody receiving the maximum.

And they were called the cuts because that was exactly what they often did to your backside. It depended on the skill or the enthusiasm of the inflicter. If he could hit the same spot each time he would draw blood. He had succeeded in giving you the cuts and had done his job effectively.

I got one dose of three and two of two during my time at the Prince of Wales. The dose of three was inflicted on me only eleven days after I arrived at school – I cannot remember the offence but I do remember that it was a mild one and I suspect it was the policy to give a fair number of rabbles a dose of the cane early on just to remind them of who was boss.

I accepted it as part of the learning process, the initiation ceremony; I suspect it was a bit of a psychological shock to many others who were away from home for the first time and were already finding it difficult to adjust to their strange new surroundings.

To receive your punishment you were ushered into the prefects' room – most of the prefects were usually present – and you were told to bend down and, with both hands, touch the rugby ball on the floor in front of you.

Then you were caned. The prefect either stood close to you and raised his arm but some actually took a three-yard run at you to inflict the maximum pain. The prefects watched closely to see how you reacted – if you blubbed the whole school would eventually know. Some guys must have had leather backsides because they marched out of the prefects' room with insolent smiles on their faces. Others blubbed effusively. I remember I kept a straight face but there were no smiles – if I looked too cocky or unruffled they might try harder the next time. The prospect of the cuts always scared the hell out of me.

In the same week that I had my dose of three cuts I suffered another dose of humiliation. One evening I was summoned into the prefects' room and told I was in charge of the gramophone, which meant having to put the records on and wind it up. One of the records was called, or had the refrain, 'I'm a hula-hula-hula girl'. I was ordered to dance to that tune time and time again, gyrating and twisting like a worm on a pin while they laughed and yelled. To protest too much or give the hint of insolence invited the cuts so I preferred the indignity of the hula-hula girl any time.

The diary for that day states: 'In the morning I had prep and swat. I went to the library. At night I had to dance for the prefects.' I made it sound like an everyday occurrence, like the sort of thing any twelve-year-old would do at the end of a school day. That humiliation and the fact that I had the cuts in only my second week at school made demands on my resilience and, fortunately, I had plenty. Somewhere deep down a voice must have been saying to me, 'Don't let the bastards get you down.' And I didn't.

There were other little chores expected of the rabble. I had to make a prefect's bed and change his sheets once a week. I also had to do my weekly stint of washing his jockstrap. (The temptation to put itching powder in it was always resisted by me, the devout coward; others did not have the same will power and we all enjoyed the hilarity that followed, safe in the knowledge that we would not suffer the cuts that would inevitably be the outcome for the perpetrator).

We had to take turns at doing the week's trades – setting the tables at meal times and tidying up afterwards. This meant getting up at 6.30 instead of 7 and having to move pretty quickly after the meal to keep up with the timetable.

The entire routine revolved around learning, either in the wooden classrooms or at prep in the common rooms, and sport. And, of course, food, of which we could never get enough. I arrived at school as a slightly pampered wee lad who was able to turn his nose up at certain vegetables. Not at the Prince of Wales – you were hungry enough to eat any vegetable that they put in front of you and my liking for vegetables of any kind remains more than half a century later. But all the bread we were offered was brown bread (unless you were a prefect) and to this day I can't stand brown bread.

Each weekday morning started with the assembly in the school chapel. Before the morning service got under way the headmaster would make various announcements. The Jews and the Catholics were not allowed to attend what was a religious assembly and no doubt did not want to; they had to huddle outside the front door to hear what the headmaster had to say then they would shuffle away like pariahs while we got on worshipping our God our way.

Every Wednesday there was a shopping lorry. This took about twenty of us into Nairobi for the afternoon. To be accorded this privilege, this brief bout of freedom, you had to fill in an application form stating exactly the purpose of your visit to the town – a haircut, a birthday present, a personal purchase. Your request was not always granted – it was often just a skive anyway but as long as you did not make too many outrageous requests you were seldom knocked back.

When you were in town you were still officially at school, representing the school, so you had to be on your best behaviour. The man to watch out for was the gym teacher, Johnny Riddell, a Scot. If he caught you with your hands in your pockets you did twenty press-ups on the spot. He caught me early on and I did twenty press-ups on the pavement outside the posh New Stanley Hotel in the centre of the city.

I got to know that pavement well – years later on that same spot as a reporter with the *East African Standard* I interviewed William Holden and Mary Pickford. And at a table about twenty yards from that spot Edward G Robinson made clandestine plans for a meeting with my dad.

I had worn spectacles since I was about eighteen months old so you would think I would be able to look after them. Far from it. Constantly losing or breaking my glasses was one of the hazards of my young life. I did not need them for playing sport and, of course, did not wear them swimming, so they often left behind the goal post or lost in the sand.

Losses and breakages meant money. Mum and Dad had bought me rimless plastic spectacles and I thought I looked pretty nifty in them. They cost £6, which was a lot of money in those days. I had to get them repaired not long after and Dad had made it clear to me that he was not at all pleased with this carelessness.

The next term at school the glasses suffered what turned out to be a terminal accident. I took them to the optician in Nairobi – three cheers for the shopping lorry – and he said he could patch them up but I would have to get a new pair. Panic. I couldn't write home with the news.

That was when I showed a bit of entrepreneurial flair which has seldom visited me since. I decided I would raise the money myself. First of all, I held a raffle. Mum was always sending me goodies – the latest was a large, sumptuous cake. This was the first prize in the raffle. And the second was a bottle of tomato sauce – we did not get that at school and Mum had also sent it to me.

That, believe it or not, raised half the money. To bring in the rest I started a library – I was proud of my collection of Sexton Blake books and I had many others – so I loaned them out for a small fee each week. It all worked amazingly well – most of the guys knew why I was doing this and there might well have been a bit of sympathetic support but few of them had more money than I had. I had noticed that the 'stinkers' took out a lot of the books – perhaps they told their parents when they went home about my fund-raising efforts and they decided covertly to help.

The outcome was that I comfortably raised the £6 and was able to buy myself a new pair of plastic spectacles. I somehow let this information slip when I went home at the end of the term and got hell from my parents for not telling them. I felt I could not win – but I think they must have been secretly proud of my efforts.

During my time at the Prince of Wales, a State of Emergency was declared in Kenya (20 October 1952) as the brutal Mau Mau terrorist organisation pressed its claim for an independent Kenya. The State of Emergency ended in January 1960 and during that terrible conflict thousands of black Kenyans were killed by both sides and thirty-two white settlers were killed by terrorists – and the sons of some of the butchered settlers were at the school.

This inevitably meant tight security at school and it was not unusual to find in the morning that all of the African staff had been taken by the police for questioning after some terrorist activity, usually a murder. The situation at the school was described thus in the school magazine:

> Security precautions against terrorist activities are being carefully maintained. A post of regular police has been established in the school compound for some time now. These, in conjunction with the school watchmen, maintain day and night patrols.

In addition, mobile patrols, composed of members of staff, do duty at night. Many of the buildings are now surrounded by barbed wire fencing so that, altogether, we feel reasonably well protected.

We noticed the change and felt the tension on our shopping lorry trips into town. Most of the whites, men and women, were carrying firearms and more police than usual, all heavily armed, were in evidence.

For those of us whose homes were outside Kenya there was little to worry about the safety of our parents, who were certainly concerned about our safety as atrocities against blacks and whites continued to dominate the headlines.

For others, there was a two-way worry. Those who lived on outlying farms in Kenya were principal targets for the Mau Mau. While naturally concerned about their own safety they were worried about their children at the Prince of Wales. So it was a trying time all round.

I saw at first hand the tragedy of it all. One of my mates was Sergio Beccaloni, and on Sunday night he was quietly summoned from the school dining room by the headmaster. There was a stunned silence from us all as, instinctively, we knew that it was bad news. Sergio's father had been brutally slashed to death at his farm by the Mau Mau.

Fortunately, that was the only serious incursion the Emergency made into school life, although a teacher was occasionally conscripted into Emergency service and the Headmaster would now and again make an announcement about an ex-pupil who had been killed while on active service.

One letter from the Headmaster to parents stated: 'I regret that five members of my staff are to be seconded for important Emergency duties. I think we shall be able to recruit some well-qualified ladies so that we can keep classroom teaching going; but we shall sorely miss the vigour of these five men and the help they give in all manner of activities.' It was a false hope – I cannot recall any ladies at all coming to brighten up the scene.

We were used to teachers being seconded for Emergency duties – or, as we put it, to fight the Mau Mau. Security was important. The Headmaster took his instructions from the police as regards what one letter to parents called 'Boarders Leaving the Compound'. Boys will be boys and rules are there to be broken out of sheer devilment if nothing else but there was no display of bravado as regards security rules – no sneaking out to the bright lights of Nairobi. We were only too well aware of what the Mau Mau could do and we kept well within the confines of school. Besides, the Headmaster was also a formidable figure.

I was never likely to become the Brain of Britain but I was certainly better than my initial class of 1C and two terms later I was in 1A. I remained in an A class for the rest of my time at the school.

It was always important to be part of a team and I found myself very much a team player, a willing participant.

I became a member of the school brass band, graduating from the cymbals to the big bass drum then the side drum. This meant regular Saturday appearances at the school parade and also on other ceremonial occasions.

I also became a member of the Combined Cadet Force, ready to fight for king and country. I also joined the school choir, the philatelic society and even managed to get myself appointed as an assistant librarian – all part of the team spirit with a decided touch of individualism.

All of this looked pretty good on your school report, of course, but I remember one particularly glowing report from the Headmaster was accompanied by a letter to parents from him which began thus:

> The influenza epidemic disorganised work, games and other activities for the first four of five weeks of term. Since then, some unfortunate individuals have had much shorter and milder illnesses, but in general the health of the boys has been good for the second half of term.
>
> In addition to influenza among members of Staff we have had other misfortunes and teaching has suffered accordingly. Because of this, it has often been difficult, or well nigh impossible, to arrive at a correct evaluation of the work of the boy; and I fear that some end of term reports will contain marks or comments based on slender evidence.

So a crumb of comfort for those who brought home a poor report but if you flourished a glowing report at your inquiring parents there was that sting in the tale about 'slender evidence'.

On Queen's Day, 11 October 1954, the annual day for pomp and circumstance at the school, the guest of honour was Michael Blundell, who was Minister without Portfolio. In his address he told us we that we could divorce Africa from the events of the world.

He stated: 'In this struggle between what is right for Man and what is wrong, Africa has a vital role to play. This Emergency of ours is merely an indication of what is going on everywhere, very often openly in other continents but certainly secretly and latently all over Africa.'

Prophetic words from a man who also had a vital role ahead of him. He was six years later to form the New Kenya Party which recognised the need to join the African in an independent Kenya. He was regarded by most Europeans as a traitor to his kind, but he was actually a brave man ahead of his time.

I was to hear him speak again more than six years later when, as an *East African Standard* reporter, I covered a meeting in Nyeri as the political situation started to heat up in the long run-in to internal self-government and independence.

But when I heard him that Queen's Day in October I had nine days previously received that telegram from Dad telling me that I was starting as a sports reporter with the *Tanganyika Standard* on 4 January.

I was well prepared. Earlier that year, in what was a legacy of that first year I had spent in Dar es Salaam with no schooling, I had realised that I was far behind with my three science subjects and had no chance of passing them in the Cambridge Overseas School Certificate examinations at the end of 1954.

I managed to persuade the Headmaster, Philip Fletcher, that instead of going to science classes I should be allowed to repair to the library and teach myself shorthand. This was a highly unusual request, to say the least. It meant putting a lot of trust in me and letting me get on with it. He gave me permission, not without hesitation, and I recall on several occasions thereafter the silence of the library being disturbed by the door being slowly opened and Mr Fletcher peering in over his spectacles just to check that I was there. I certainly was – I had invested in Teach Yourself Pitman's Shorthand and was diligently applying myself to the task.

I practised taking down the words of popular songs – Kitty Kallen's 'Little Things Mean a Lot', a nice, slow ballad, was my first exercise in shorthand and I thereafter started to practise on the radio news.

By the time I heard Michael Blundell on that Queen's Day I was able to take a few notes in shorthand for the house magazine, the *Clive House Chinwag*, which I had started that year.

It was handwritten by me each week with one of the lads drawing a cartoon or two to brighten it up and I covered sporting events and general school activities such as the speech by Michael Blundell and an earlier one by Dr L S B Leakey. After it had been approved by the House Master, the magazine was left in the common room for all to read. And it was well received.

So my first shorthand reporting job was Michael Blundell in the *Clive House Chinwag*. I was getting ready for my entry into the newspaper world when I left school at the end of that year.

There was, however, a little unexpected hurdle ahead.

Dad had followed up his telegram with a letter in which he told me more about what lay ahead with the *Tanganyika Standard*. I was to get a salary of £20 a month for the first six months then move on to £25. When I got home I would have to meet the Managing Director of the *Tanganyika Standard* and, although the job was mine, I would still have to make a good impression.

Dad's letter went on: 'So, lad, you have got a start. Your mum is highly delighted and, of course, so am I. Kelman tells me you have got a fancy haircut – well, all I can say is don't come home like that as you will have to meet this man.'

My goose was cooked! On one of the shopping lorry trips into Nairobi I had been foolish enough to get myself a crew cut, which was the rage of the time (quite unlike me, in fact, to run with the herd). But I felt I cut quite a dash with my rimless specs and my new hairstyle.

Now I was soon to go home to face Dad and the managing director of the *Tanganyika Standard* with this way out, trendy hair cut. How long does it take for a crew cut to grow out? Could I get away with a hat?

I was in despair. I had the ambition. I had launched a handwritten house magazine. I had already reported the words of a leading Kenya politician. At the age of sixteen I had shorthand.

But I also had a crew cut.

THE SODDEN EMBRACE OF THE RUFIJI – WHERE EVEN A FUGITIVE WOULD NOT SEEK ASYLUM

The *Tanganyika Standard* was the English-language newspaper of what was then known as Tanganyika Territory. It was in the same group as the *Mombasa Times*, the *Uganda Argus* in Kampala and the flagship, the *East African Standard* in Nairobi.

It was read by just about every European in Dar es Salaam. Sometimes it was a pretty thin offering, but on other days it had a fairly healthy thump as it hit the table or the floor. It had to balance news coverage between what was happening in Tanganyika and the rest of East Africa and what was happening in the UK – regarded as home by most of its readers.

All its journalists had served their time mainly on newspapers in the UK and were men and women of experience. Most were on contracts from the United Kingdom, as was the practice with most companies and Government departments in East Africa, and the newspaper did not take on trainees. But, thanks to the influence that I know Dad and his friends were able to exert, I became the *Tanganyika Standard*'s first trainee journalist.

My newspaper life started on Monday, 3 January 1956. I was dressed in a white shirt, white shorts, long white stockings, black crepe-soled shoes and, of course, my rimless specs. I had somehow managed to clear the crew cut hurdle – the managing director had a bit of a hairstyle himself – and I was definitely looking older than my years, which has been a drawback or an asset all my life.

By then we had moved from Oyster Bay into Smuts Street in the centre of Dar and the *Tanganyika Standard* office was not far away. Distance did not matter – I had wheels. Two of them. My own bike. I was without doubt a journalist on the move.

The editor of the *Standard* was a gentleman of the old school,

Oswald 'Ozzie' Blake. He was respected by all the staff; a short man with a moustache, and while white shorts were the norm among the journalists, Ozzie always favoured long whites.

Although I must have been something of an inconvenience and perhaps an imposition he did not show it. He gave me a warm welcome that first day and constant encouragement throughout my stay. From day one he sat me beside his secretary, Ann Thomas, at a desk opposite his room.

We were separated by a translucent glass partition and every so often Ozzie would appear clutching a piece of paper, spectacles low on the nose, and wander through to the newsroom with a suggestion or an instruction. By mid-afternoon you could hear the tip tap of his typewriter and you knew that tomorrow's leader was being carefully crafted.

For me it was a little while before I got the typewriter tapping. Although that historic telegram from Dad had said that I was to be a sports reporter that was not the case. When I did get a chance to do some reporting it was as general and basic as could be, with sport only an occasional part of it.

In the meantime my first few weeks were spent filing photographs and the metal blocks of photographs that had been published. This was not as boring as it sounds – the photographs were supplied by international news agencies and reading the captions provided a useful education in current affairs and personalities. I also became an avid reader of *Keesing's Contemporary Archives*.

Soon I graduated to taking messages off the teleprinter and I did some proofreading. Then I was allowed to accompany one of the reporters as he went his daily rounds to the District Commissioner's office, Government departments, the courts and the police, picking up bits of information, having a chat and a cup of coffee – this was not the heady, hold-the-front-page stuff. There was no need to hold the front page anyway – there was no opposition, there was no circulation battle.

My introduction to the newspaper world was undoubtedly a civilised and gentle one but I was not getting into print quickly enough for my liking and my burgeoning ambition. My diary entry for 25 January: 'Wrote a short story on cinema censorship.

Look forward to tomorrow – story in the paper!' No, it wasn't – what experience or qualification I had then, or even now, to write about cinema censorship I do not know, but at least the *Tanganyika Standard* readers were spared the benefits of the dubious knowledge on the subject from a seventeen-year-old.

26 January: 'Did a story for Mr Blake about a sheikh's son dieing [sic] in Zanzibar. Approved – and in the paper tomorrow.' No, it wasn't – the sheikh's son might have deserved a place in our columns, but this task had fallen into the hands of somebody who could not even spell 'dying', so how could he look after an obituary?

I kept on trying. I still have the handwritten first efforts – they did not make it to the pages of the newspaper and did not even make the typewriter. They were snippets I picked up from the police incident book and I would cycle back to the office feverishly and eagerly to write them out and then, despairingly, to find them being turned down or just tactfully put into a drawer with nothing said.

'Don't even bother to type them – you're not ready yet,' I was told.

The 'trainee' part of my job hardly applied. I can recall only once being taken aside and given some advice on how to write a news story; mostly it was a case of learning by myself and that did not worry me because I had plenty of enthusiasm and a reasonable helping of confidence.

Unwanted though my early efforts might have been as far as I was concerned they did not deserve to end up in the bucket. I invariably managed to retrieve the handwritten snippets and I have kept them in a folder since 1955, souvenirs of those early days when I eagerly awaited publication of what I thought was vital information for *Tanganyika Standard* readers but got no further than the subeditor's table.

Here are some examples of essential tidings that were by that process withheld from the Tanganyika public:

Miss H B Bhatt was robbed of her gold necklace at the junction of Kisutu-Ingles Street yesterday morning. The thief is believed to have been an African wearing a red-and-black striped shirt.

This could have been the world's first mugging yet the *Tanganyika Standard* ignored the scoop.

> At Uma River recently an elderly herdsman died from injuries sustained in an attack by a stock thief, who hit him on the head with a stick. The identity of the murderer is known but an arrest has not yet been made.

A murderous – and apparently not anonymous – stick stock thief was on the loose but the public were not told.

> Selemani Sultani was sentenced to 21 months' hard labour at the Dar es Salaam Magistrate's Court for assault and stealing goods valued at forty shillings. The accused, who pleaded not guilty, was disturbed while entering a house at Mnazi Moja. He then drew a penknife and attacked an African.

A disturbed thief on the prowl with a vicious penknife – but that news was not allowed to disturb the readers of the *Tanganyika Standard*.

But my debut publication day was getting close. I kept on plugging away and on 1 February 1955, I finally made it. The story was heavily subbed to make it understandable, but this was no epic about pioneering muggers, murderous stick-carrying men or disturbed thieves armed to the teeth with a penknife.

This Dow first told the readers:

> About 20 per cent of the total number of telephone exchange lines at present in commission in Tanganyika were installed last year, according to an official of the E A Posts and Telecommunications.

There were seven more paragraphs in similar vein. Was this deemed to be what the public had been waiting to learn? It was actually across two columns, so it must have been important, I reasoned, and considering how much of my material had so far been rejected the fact that it was used meant it must have been good.

So I reckoned I had made it. I was ready for anything. The next assignment was the annual general meeting of the Dar es

Salaam Horticultural Society and I did not miss a trick. I had to swallow hard – I had to give up playing that evening for the Gymkhana Club in their opening football match of the season, by no means the last time in my career that football and work were to clash and the latter win.

The resulting story from this important horticultural event was across only a single column, but at least the public, thanks to my sacrificial endeavours, now knew that Mr John Roper (yes, the husband of the lady who had been in charge of my exam for the Prince of Wales School in the comfort of her Oyster Bay house) was now the President of the Dar es Salaam Horticultural Society and the Vice-President was no less a personage than Mr N R Fuggles-Couchman. Yes, forget the muggings and assaults and the murder of the old cattleman somewhere up-country – this was what the folk in Dar wanted to read about.

Soon the Editor had enough confidence in me to let me cover the courts on my own and I picked up enough snippets of interest to help build up my precious collection of cuttings.

Looking at them now I cannot help but be struck by the incongruity of it all. I am sure that those dispensing justice did it to the best of their ability with fairness very much in mind but in the Tanganyika of the '50s justice was rough and tough and not always consistent.

A man was given a three-year sentence for what was described as the defilement of a girl under twelve years of age. The magistrate said the accused had a shocking record and had to be put away for a while.

Another was sentenced to two years' hard labour for the indecent assault of a four-year-old girl. The magistrate's comments are worth recording for a second time: 'This is a heavy punishment but it is nothing compared with the penalties suffered in European countries for similar offences in days when they were emerging from barbarism.'

So they seemed reasonably severe with child molesters and I have no quarrel with that.

But a few days later I reported that an individual called Muhidini Jumanne had been sentenced to two years to be followed by three years of police supervision – for stealing a bicycle. He'd stolen twice before and that was obviously enough to put him on a par with a child molester.

A couple of thieves who knocked somebody out and stole his wristwatch were given three years each. No previous convictions were notified, but the prosecutor was able to damn them anyway by being allowed to state that there had been a lot of trouble in the area and this had decreased since the two men had been arrested.

One thing which struck me was that all the court activity concerned Africans and occasionally Asians. Europeans did not seem to get into trouble – were we really all law-abiding citizens or did our benevolent colonial police force turn a blind eye if the white man transgressed?

There were one or two instances when visiting white sailors would get into a brawl and end up in court but they were not locals so somehow this did not impugn on the Dar European population who remained pillars of rectitude and were thus able to show the inferior African that the white man did not break the law.

My court duties were interrupted one day with words that sent a chill down my spine: 'I want you to go to St Joseph's Convent.'

Back flooded five-year-old bitter memories of my first few days in Dar. But this time the words were uttered by the editor, Ozzie Blake, and he wanted me to go to investigate a tip-off that some old German relics had been discovered during building work at the school.

So it was back to the dreaded St Joseph's Convent, this time not with a schoolbag and a heavy heart but carrying a notebook and pencil and what I hoped was an air of authority.

I returned to the office with enough information to merit four paragraphs. Workmen on an extension to the convent had unearthed an old German letter box, believed to be more than forty-nine years old, and it was now destined for the local museum. Hardly ancient relics, but it has to be remembered that we were short on historical material in Dar and there was a particular fascination with the country's Germanic past.

Tanganyika – or German East Africa as it was then known – had figured prominently in the First World War. It was here that the Allied forces encountered the most determined colonial opposition under the leadership of the legendary Lt (later Major General) Paul von Lettow-Vorbeck.

With a combination of guile and military skill he held out against opponents throughout the war and was able to bottle up 300,000 Allied troops needed elsewhere. The fighting in German East Africa merits little space in most volumes of the First World War, regarded, wrongly, as a bit of a sideshow, but the British–German struggle in Tanganyika was significant in East African terms.

In many ways von Lettow-Vorbeck pioneered guerrilla warfare and is still regarded as one of the greatest guerrilla leaders in history. He and his jungle troops – Germans and local tribesmen – had fought off overwhelming superior forces – more than 150,000 Allied troops and one million military – and were still unassailable weeks after the war was over. When he heard that hostilities had ceased and that Germany was on the losing side Lettow-Vorbeck smartened up his troops and marched them to the nearest British garrison and, observing the strict military discipline which was his hallmark, he officially handed over his sword in surrender.

The British commander, who knew so well the exploits of this man who, with a force considerably inferior in number, had frustrated the might of the British army for so long, said: 'My dear sir, you were never defeated. You don't have to surrender.'

I'd already read an account of von Lettow-Vorbeck's Tanganyika campaign and had a keen interest in relics of the time, even if it meant going back to St Joseph's Convent.

Soon I blossomed beyond the four-paragraph stories and started to write feature length pieces. I had a healthy inquisitiveness and I think I impressed my superiors by my tenacity and my determination to produce material.

When we had lived in Oyster Bay on the outskirts of Dar we got there from the main town by driving across Selander Bridge. On working days it was at least twice a day because everybody went home for lunch and forty winks. Dad had it down to a fine art – he could be across that bridge and in his bed for his siesta twenty-five minutes after the noon start of the two-hour lunch break and that was in the not-too-speedy Bessie.

So who was Selander? I was determined to find out. My research showed that his full name was John Einar Selander, who had been Director of Public Works in Dar in 1923. The town then was growing rapidly and Selander built that bridge to get the stone from Msasani at the other side to help build Dar. So the bridge had been constructed to meet the needs of the expanding Dar round the harbour and not to develop houses on the other side.

Hardly world-shattering, but the people of Dar did not know this and my feature was prominently displayed with my byline.

At the entrance to Dar harbour was the Makatumbe lighthouse. We all knew it was there and saw it every night – but how long had it been there? Since 1894, in fact, and the Germans had managed to put it temporarily out of action during the First World War. I dug up enough information to provide a useful feature.

The cuttings collection was growing, and by the time I had put in my first full year with the paper I was ready for the great adventure which was to come my way – courtesy of a mild, mannered, shy tree expert from Edinburgh.

Bill Finlayson was Tanganyika's Assistant Conservator of Forests and was a friend of the family. He was based in the Rufiji Delta, 100 miles down the coast, and on one of his visits to Dar he popped in to tell us that he would soon be collecting the Forestry Department's first motor launch to help him with his work in the Rufiji, Tanganyika's chief river.

He suggested that it would be a good idea if I came with him to cover the event for the *Tanganyika Standard*. Apart from the enjoyable experience, he reckoned there might be a feature or two in it. He thought it would do my nascent journalistic career no harm and the Forestry Department would welcome the publicity.

I agreed with him, and I was elated – and more than a little surprised – to find that I quickly had Ozzie Blake's support for the venture. I think my zeal in producing features was a big factor. He then gilded the lily by saying that the newspaper would make the necessary arrangements to fly me back.

So at ten minutes to four on the morning of 1 February 1956, the alarm clock bell went off and I was quickly out of bed. I grabbed my case and Dad drove me down to the harbour to meet Bill. I knew that my parents were a bit uneasy about me disappearing into part of the unknown of Africa with this quiet fellow Scot but at seventeen going on eighteen I was keen and determined and there was no stopping me.

So the three-ton launch Mkulukala, with Bill at the helm, and me on the deck to enjoy the sunrise, glided out of Dar es Salaam harbour at 5.25 a.m. and headed for the open Indian Ocean.

Our destination was Dima, a little peninsula at the southern tip of the Rufiji Delta, which was Bill's base for his work in the mangrove swamps. It had been chosen because of its very good water supply and the easy access to the island of Mafia ten miles way.

Twelve hours after our departure we entered the Rufiji Delta. The delta has been described by Elspeth Huxley thus:

> Lying in a sodden embrace of mud and mangrove trees, it is a morass of serpentine creeks and brackish tidal channels, clogged with sandbars, writhing with crocodiles, snarling with mosquitoes, trembling with the crash of elephant herds in the matted rain forests around its banks.
>
> The delta does not welcome man; one almost expects to find rubbery prehistoric animals wallowing about in its miasma. It breathes isolation and spawns disease. Even a fugitive would hesitate before seeking asylum here.

I was no fugitive, just a starry-eyed seventeen-year-old reporter with a baby Brownie and a portable typewriter. Had my parents been able to read Elspeth Huxley's description of the horrors of the Rufiji Bill Finlayson would have been told politely to paddle his own canoe.

The Rufiji River must surely be one of the greatest rivers in Africa. It is 400 miles long and the delta itself encompasses an area roughly the size of metropolitan New York.

At one time it was reputed that seventy-five per cent of its teeming crocodile population had skins which were affected by what was called 'buttons'. This was a strange lump in the middle of the scale which prevented proper tanning. That should have been enough to save them from the hunters but it was not; they shot them in the name of sport anyway. Yet there were still a few around as the Mkulukala eased her way up the river.

Just before dusk we approached an imposing Arab dhow, which was anchored up the river, waiting to collect mangrove poles. (About a hundred years earlier it would have been trying to avoid British ships while it picked up another cargo of slaves). This dhow was to be our venue for dinner that evening – surely the first time a Dow has dined on a dhow?

Bill was an old friend of the pilot – Mbarak Said Marzuk – and we scrambled on board to meet him. He was a fine figure, tall and stately with a well-trimmed beard and he came forward to greet us and to introduce us to the captain. Bill was well known to them as Bwana Miti (trees) and I was introduced simply as Bwana Mgeni (stranger).

We sat down cross-legged, on a beautiful carpet and comfortable cushions at the stern of the ship, which was raised above the level of the deck. At a brisk word of command food was brought to us by an Arab boy who could not have been more than ten years old.

We were served from a big tray with several Arab dishes, such as halwa, an Arabian version of Turkish Delight. This was followed by tea then coffee.

After this snack, Mbarak produced a thick volume of *Norie's Nautical Tables*, a sextant and aged charts and asked us to explain some of the signs and words used in the book. Most of the data in the book was beyond us, but Bill managed somehow and when it started getting really difficult for him he turned the tables on Mbarak by asking him to explain the method he used to pilot the ship from Bombay to Zanzibar and this pleased him greatly.

During the conversation I learned that the dhow had travelled without cargo from Muscat to Mangalore, where they collected the tiles they were going to sell, and eventually reached Zanzibar twenty-five days later. They had sold their tiles in Dar and were now in the Rufiji to collect their mangrove poles.

Mbarak insisted that we should stay for the main meal, which was curried chicken. During the meal we had to strictly observe what I was told were Arab customs, such as eating food with the right hand only and always drinking three cups of coffee – no more, no less.

During the meal, the pilot excused himself and went to join the rest of the crew who were conducting the evening prayer. He returned soon afterwards and told us he had arranged a special dance in our honour.

Drums and a bell were quickly produced and the Arabs stood in a circle, singing and beating rhythmically with their feet and hands, displaying amazing precision and timing.

Very soon a man appeared dressed as a woman and picked a partner from the circle of men. The beating of the drums grew faster and louder as the two dancers sinuated and teased each other. The dhow was lit only by a hurricane lamp, which swung to and fro above the dancers, barely illuminating the excited, sweaty faces of the energetic performers and their enthusiastic onlookers while casting weird and grotesque shadows over the ship.

Mbarak explained that the dance portrayed a woman resisting the intentions of her partner until she is eventually won over to the cheers and the whoops of the entire crew.

For this seventeen-year-old innocent scribe who thought that a chaste cheek-to-cheek dance was sexual nirvana, this was pretty heady stuff. Wait till I tell the boys back in Dar about this!

We tipped the leader of the dancers for his entertainment and made to leave. A brisk injunction from the captain cleared the deck of the still-panting dancers as Bwanas Miti and Mgeni made their way down the gangway, watched by dozens of peering faces over the side of the dhow.

I was a bit wobbly in the knees as we descended the gangway – that, I told myself, was because I had been sitting cross-legged for so long, and nothing else.

It was back to the good ship Mkulukala and two hours later we reached our destination for the night, Salale. As Bill put it: 'The mosquitoes are so big you can keep them out with chicken wire.' We slept under mosquito nets but the thirsty horrors still got to us.

Salale had been at the centre of a cat-and-mouse nautical game during the First World War. The German light cruiser, the *Koenigsberg*, caused the British quite a few problems up and down the East African coast, especially when it sunk the cruiser *Pegasus*.

This sinking was the first serious engagement of the First World War in East Africa. The *Koenigsberg* entered Zanzibar harbour, sank the *Pegasus*, which had put in for repairs, and made off at speed, disappearing into the Rufiji Delta and finding refuge at Salale.

When the British were trying to trace the whereabouts of the *Koenigsberg* the name 'Salale' cropped up in several German radio messages which the British intercepted but nobody had ever heard of the place so the *Koenigsberg* remained safe for another few months.

Eventually the *Koenigsberg* was blockaded in the Rufiji and was finally destroyed in July 1925 – thanks to an angry elephant hunter. His name was Pieter Pretorius and he was not too happy when his hunting lodge was commandeered by the Germans. He got his revenge by tracking down the *Koenigsberg* in the Rufiji, boarding the vessel disguised as an Arab selling chickens and he then passed the ship's position on to the British.

In a combined air and sea operation in July 1915 the *Koenigsberg* was shelled and critically damaged in what was a bloody battle for the Germans and was finally scuttled by her badly wounded captain, Max Looff. Until floods broke up the remains of the ship in 1978 her listing tunnels could clearly be seen above the water.

But after the daring deed by Pieter Pretorius parts of the *Koenigsberg* remained to fight on.

The *Koenigsberg* had a sting in her tail. It had lost twenty-three of her crew who were killed and thirty-five were wounded but it had not lost its massive guns and they were destined to continue to play an important part in the war. The resourceful von Lettow-Vorbeck managed to get her guns and used them to augment his artillery. Getting them off the wreck was a massive effort in itself but they were then taken overland to Dar – it is reckoned that between 300 and 400 African labourers were involved but they made it and thereafter the guns were called into action for the rest of the campaign. They represented the heaviest artillery in the East African campaign – it seems hard to believe that after successfully hunting down the *Koenigsberg* the British did not see the value of these guns, which von Lettow-Vorbeck clearly did. Of the *Koenigsberg*'s total crew of 350, only fifteen, including Captain Looff, survived the war and made it back to Germany.

Not far from where we moored for the night after our Arab dhow hospitality was the wreck of the supply ship *Somali*, which had been trying to get to the *Koenigsberg* before the British got to her.

We passed the wreck in the morning and sailed up the delta and eventually to Dima, where Bill's wife, June, and the local workforce were waiting. We tied up at a wooden jetty to loud shouts and cheers. I felt I had wandered into a Hollywood movie and if a David Livingstone lookalike had been there waiting for me I would not have been the least bit surprised.

Waiting for me instead was Nicholas, a donkey. It was a bit of a safari through the mangrove bush to get to the Finlayson homestead and they had decided that I should be given the honour of having the travelling services of Nicholas.

Nicholas did not see it as an honour – I spent the journey trying to swat off a nasty variety of persistent and aggressive insects which found this newcomer very tasty while at the same time trying to avoid the constant attempts by Nicholas to bite me. Whether winged or four-legged they wanted a chunk of me at Dima.

There was more to come.

The Finlayson household was still being built and most of the workforce was prison labour. That did not really worry me. But it had been a long day and I was ready for an early night in a comfortable bed. That did not bother my hosts because they understood it had been a bit of a journey, but any hopes I had about being ushered into a comfortable bedroom and an equally comfortable bed were quickly dashed.

Bill took me to the front door, pointed into the darkness and said, 'Have a good sleep – you'll find your tent down there.' He handed me an oil lamp with a light which was flickering in the evening breeze. This was to help me find my way, he explained, and he counselled, 'Keep it on all night.'

'Why?' I asked.

'It'll scare any wandering hippos away,' he said.

I found the tent in the middle of the pitch dark African night and stumbled over a camp bed which was fully six inches off the ground. There was also a small table and chair and, tired though I was, I was not in a hurry to lie down and place myself at the disposal of a meandering hippo. So I carefully rested the precious lamp on the table, opened my portable typewriter, gingerly sat down, all the while anxiously looking around me and started to type out my first notes on this memorable safari.

But the light, which would supposedly keep a hippo at bay, attracted a wide variety of bugs and mosquitoes, and around 10.50 I had to give in. I got down to virtual ground level on the camp bed, made sure the mosquito net was safely tucked in, saw reassuringly that the oil lamp was still on and went to sleep.

It was the howling wind which wakened me. And to my horror I quickly realised that it was pitch dark. The oil lamp had gone out. Despite the mosquito net I had been bitten to hell. And there was a creature at the bottom of the bed sniffing and snorting and slowly progressing along the length of the camp bed in my direction.

There's not much in a seventeen-year-old life to flash past your eyes but what I had certainly flashed past mine. I lay there absolutely terrified, while this creature's sniffing and snorting worked their way up the bed towards my petrified face. Of course it was sniffing and snorting – that's what a dog does, isn't it? A 3 a.m. bedside visit by a dog had never been more welcome.

I was not too chirpy in the morning. There was a long day ahead and a houseboy wakened me at 5.15 with a cup of tea. The diary states: 'As I took that cup of tea the mosquitoes were still eating me alive. I rushed into the house and sat on the settee. I felt terrible. My upper lip and chin were swollen considerably. I just sat in agony. When I got up to go I could hardly stand on my feet I was so dizzy. I had to sit down for another spell then shakily made a move.'

Ahead was a two-and-a-half hour journey in the launch to the island of Mafia, where we met the District Commissioner, Donald B Cameron. Then we had another hour's journey to meet an Arab friend of Bill's and he entertained us to black coffee, coconuts and cashew nuts. Another hour and we were back at base. The mosquitoes had missed me and were pleased to see me back. To this day I do not know how I did not get malaria.

Social life in the Rufiji was hardly hectic but there was one evening I will never forget. I dined with Rufiji.

'Rufiji' was the pseudonym used by R de la B Barker for pieces he wrote in the *Tanganyika Standard*. He was something of a mystery character but the story is that in 1930, having lost all his worldly possessions, he spent his first lonely season in a hermitage in the Rufiji, isolated by seasonal floods.

Natives who knew him as an elephant hunter turned to him to kill marauding hippos and he settled down to a life in small grass huts or hermitages in areas of forest, river, lake, swamp, tidal creek, hill and mountain – always teeming with life in various forms.

He put on paper his observations about creatures large and small and about the Africans themselves. His first articles appeared in the *Tanganyika Standard* in 1931. In 1944 a selection of his articles was published in a rare book entitled *The Crowded Life of a Hermit* and I am privileged to have a copy.

On the flyleaf the publishers state:

> Every incident in the book is vibrant with life. A sense of vital movement pervades its pages. Every happening is an absorbing crisis in the history of some creature, no matter how small and insignificant to all but the searching and understanding eye of a hermit.
>
> Testimony to his success in picturing what he has seen is implicit in the impressive record of sales of his work in East Africa alone. In Tanganyika and contiguous territories he is an institution. He has been called The Thoreau of Africa.

This man had spent twenty-six years living as a hermit in the Rufiji. I'd had a couple of days there and was wondering how I was going to survive. Bill took me to his place for dinner and he sat in a dimly lit hut at the head of a long table in full dinner dress with African servants on either side. It was a privilege to listen to him and to meet him and he wished me well in my future career. His parting gift was a large 1950 map of Tanganyika – in those days it was just a large piece of paper to take home; now I regard it as a valued historical document. I've since had it lovingly framed and it now hangs in the entrance hall of my house.

On my final day we sailed for the island of Mafia, which sits at the mouth of the Rufiji River. The name has nothing to do with the Italian crime syndicate – I learned that it could have an Arab derivation or it was a contraction of a Swahili phrase meaning a healthy place in which to live.

It was certainly a fascinating place – as the launch slowly approached the shore in the blistering sun I marvelled at the clear, blue water and the vista of colours beneath the surface. Mafia has since become a favourite haunt of big game fishermen and scuba divers for whom the record catches and resplendent coral make it a water sports paradise.

I had managed to arrange a stay in what was known as the Government Rest House, and during the day I lashed out ten shillings on a taxi to take me to a coconut plantation to meet two Government scientists who were carrying out experiments in the air spraying of coconut plantations to try to eradicate a coconut pest which was causing a lot of problems. I had heard about them from the District Commissioner and they were somewhat surprised that a reporter had tracked them down.

They could hardly believe that I was just passing by, but they were happy enough to tell me about what they were up to and the paper carried a piece on their experiments when I got back.

The taxi took me back that evening to the rest house in Mafia and on the table in the sparsely furnished room a pencilled note was waiting for me. It said: 'Please excuse scrawl, but would you dine with us tonight? If all right, please come at 7.30. Yrs Donald B Cameron, DC.'

Dinner with the Mafia DC and his wife? A treat indeed after the Spartan life of the Rufiji, and they made me very welcome. The DC told my inquiring mind more about Mafia and was able to add more to my *Koenigsberg* story. It seems that Mafia made history in 1915 when the British used it as the first place in Africa to launch assembled planes for reconnaissance missions. Their greatest success was finding the *Koenigsberg*.

So when I flew out of Mafia and over the Rufiji I looked down on the scene of what had been an unusual, cat-and-mouse game of the First World War, which was finally settled thanks to an island which sounded like a refuge for Italian gangsters.

My flight to Dar took forty-five minutes and was a rough journey. I had spent six nights in a part of Africa where, if you remember the earlier quote from Elspeth Huxley, even a fugitive would hesitate before seeking asylum, and I topped it off with a night on the enchanting island of Mafia.

I could hardly wait to get back to the office and start typing. I was given a warm welcome back at the office, was closely questioned by the Editor about what I had been up to and told him I had enough material for a couple of features – plus photographs I had taken. A week later the paper published the first bylined feature and the second a day later, complete with a couple of photographs I had taken.

After a year in the *Standard* my cuttings book was filling up handsomely and the two Rufiji spreads were the splendid highlights.

But there would not be any more *Tanganyika Standard* cuttings. My parents were reaching the end of their second three-year tour and were going back to the UK on leave.

The *Tanganyika Standard* had been very good to me and had given me a great start to my journalistic career but we all knew the way to further this was to return to the UK.

My parents would be coming back to East Africa – to Nairobi, as it transpired – but I would be fleeing the family nest and going solo.

We flew out of Dar on 4 April 1956. The first port of call was Entebbe in Uganda and by the time we reached London we had been flying for twenty-nine hours.

Bill Taylor, the Chief Sub on the *Standard*, had given me an introduction to the Chief Reporter of *The Scotsman* in Edinburgh and I fervently hoped that this would be my first foot on the ladder of a newspaper career in the UK.

Well, I did eventually join *The Scotsman*, but that was eight years later.

I still had to go into Africa again.

THE DUST OF AFRICA IS HARD TO SHAKE OFF

I remember a reporter at his farewell presentation in Nairobi at the *East African Standard* before he returned to England saying in his broad Yorkshire accent, 'I'm going to shake the dust of Africa off my feet.'

Needless to say, he was back before he knew it. The dust of Africa is very hard to shake off.

When I left Africa for the first time after my debut stint on the *Tanganyika Standard* it was not my intention to leave for ever. Even as I flew home I was making plans to return. I had it all clearly mapped out in my mind, planned well ahead – I had to return to Scotland to work and train on a newspaper and it was my firm ambition to go back to East Africa as a fully fledged journalist.

On the final night in Dar we moved out of 14 Smuts Street and into the New Africa Hotel. My last night in Dar was 3 April 1956, and the next day we all had a big send-off at Dar airport for the first leg of our journey, which took us to Entebbe in Uganda.

The other stops were at Cairo and Rome and we landed in London twenty-nine hours after leaving Dar. Then it was back to the familiar territory of Carrick Knowe in Edinburgh, but we had a different agenda.

Mum and Dad were on the celebrated paid 'home leave'. They had four months to relax, visit friends and relatives and enjoy the new car – a Peugeot 403 – which they would take back to Africa with them.

In those four months I had to find a job. I was not in too great a hurry at first. I was keeping my hand in by doing a weekly sports column for the *Standard* back in Dar under the pseudonym of Scotia. That was keeping me in pocket money.

Then I tried them all with no luck – *The Scotsman*, the *Glasgow Herald*, the *Edinburgh Evening News*, the *Daily Express*, the *Daily Mail*. Nothing doing. I even tried D C Thomson in Dundee and was prepared to work on the *Beano* but they would not have me.

I would not say that panic was setting in – my father, mind you, was beginning to have grave doubts about my journalistic future – but I extended my search further afield and ended up by being interviewed for a job as a junior reporter on the *Galloway Gazette* in Newton Stewart in the south-west of Scotland. It was not exactly on the beaten track and my parents were not too happy at the prospect of leaving me in digs in a remote part of Scotland while they headed back to Africa. There was plenty of encouragement to come back to Africa with them but that would have been unwise and, besides, I was a stubborn guy determined to shape my own destiny.

But my parents were pleased when *The Scotsman* got back in touch with me and said that there was now a vacancy – as a copy boy. That was better as far as they were concerned – I would be safe and sound in Edinburgh with friends and relations to look after me while I learned my journalistic trade.

It was not good enough for me, though.

I knew enough about the business to realise that a copy boy was just a go-for. I, after all, had fifteen months under my belt, I had a book full of cuttings, so it was junior reporter for me in the depths of Galloway, and after an interview with the Editor in, of course, the Overseas Club in Princes Street, Edinburgh, I was soon ensconced in Newton Stewart while Mum, Dad and brothers Kelman and Irvin headed back to Africa.

As far as I was concerned Newton Stewart would be no problem – after all, I had been through the Rufiji Delta in a manner which would have impressed even Humphrey Bogart, who had done it all in *The African Queen*.

But Bogey did not have to confront my landlady. She was something else.

It was an uneasy relationship during my seven months at the *Galloway Gazette*. I enjoyed my work on the newspaper and was given increasing responsibilities which saw me covering all news and sport and even writing an extensive diary column, which was called 'Galloway Gleanings'. I also wrote a sports column under an inherited byline of Scrutator.

I managed a game or two for the local football team and

managed to cover the game for the *Gazette* as well as for the Glasgow Sunday papers. Somehow, I was never reported as having had a bad game.

My extra duties included putting an oil lamp under the radiator of the company Ford Anglia at night – that was the antifreeze in those days – and on Wednesday afternoons I had to chauffeur the editor's wife on her weekly shopping expeditions.

But the landlady situation was getting a bit tricky. I liked to stay up late at night reading and listening to the radio. That meant using electricity and that cost money. So I was told to go to bed earlier.

The landlady was deaf so how did she know when I went to bed? She could see the light under the living room door, of course. No problem – to counteract that when she went to bed I lined up cushions along the bottom of the door so that she could not see the light.

That worked for a while until she found a collaborator. A neighbour across the street also went to bed late so she undertook to tell my landlady when I put the light out. Two elderly spinsters were ganging up on me.

One night while I was writing my diary, I was being given one of the many lectures from the landlady about saving electricity and about how my deceit would not pay off because she was smarter than me and she had so many kind neighbours who would rat on me.

I told my diary that I was undergoing one of these lectures and ventured to state that if the old bugger was not so deaf I would tell her to go where it was hot.

That was it. When I came home from work at the end of the next day I was told by the landlady to pack my bags because I was being thrown out immediately. 'Why?' I asked frantically.

'Because of all those nasty things you have been writing about me in your diary,' I was told.

But I had an ace up my sleeve which I was then able to play. I was already on my way out. The *Galloway Gazette* had been good for me, certainly a lot better than being a copy boy on *The Scotsman*, but it was a bit of a backwater and I had managed to secure a job as a reporter on the *Fifeshire Advertiser* in Kirkcaldy.

I spent three years there and it was an excellent training ground.

There were two competing newspapers in the town and we all freelanced for the daily papers. So we learned how write stories for different publications and to different lengths – and at speed. I had given myself four years in Scotland because it seemed the right level of experience which would allow me to return to East Africa as a senior reporter. I also needed three years at home to sit my journalist's proficiency certificate.

The letters from Mum in Nairobi were frequent so Africa was never far from my mind. When my four years were nearly up and I had gained my proficiency certificate I wrote to the editor of the *East African Standard* and applied for a job.

The reply was quick and I was welcomed on board.

Almost four years to the day after I had left Dar I was back on a Union-Castle liner, the *Warwick Castle*, heading for East Africa for the second time, this time to start life as a senior reporter on the *East African Standard*.

The dust of Africa was still on my feet. It had all been carefully planned, my career path meticulously worked out.

But I had not been that smart. In all that careful planning I had omitted one factor – romance, which had blossomed continually with Lorna Murray after we had met at a New Year party. I had never anticipated anything other than going back to Africa on my own, so I foolishly said a fond farewell to Lorna Murray after three wonderful years and said that if we both saved up she might be able to come out to Nairobi for a holiday after perhaps a couple of years.

Yes, I was a real romantic, not exactly a fast mover.

But I redeemed myself and finally saw the light. Three months after sailing to Kenya I bought Lorna a single air fare from Edinburgh to Nairobi and sent her a bouquet with the instructions: 'Fly out in August and marry me.' Now there's romance for you!

Lorna, just nineteen, had barely been out of Edinburgh. Now she was preparing to fly to Nairobi to marry this slow-moving scribe.

Africa was about to get another convert.

'The Leader to Darkness and Death'

I had left Kenya as a schoolboy on 14 December 1954, when the country was still in the grips of the Mau Mau Emergency as the growing African nationalist movement challenged the British Government and took dreadful revenge on its own countrymen who refused to take the terrible oaths to oust and kill the white man.

The European population gritted their teeth and dug in, stalwart in the firm belief that they were defending their own country and would be keeping African rule at bay for decades.

The Kenya I returned to on 24 April 1960 was a vastly different place. The Emergency had been officially over for three mouths and the country was still reverberating from the speech by the British Prime Minister, Harold Macmillan, in Cape Town, the famous 'wind of change speech'.

The Europeans in Kenya shivered at the Macmillan words: 'The wind of change is blowing through this continent, and whether we like it or not this growth of national consciousness is a political fact – and our national policies must take account of it. We must accept it.'

This pronouncement was made a few weeks after a constitutional conference on the future of Kenya had been held at Lancaster House in London. 'The future of Kenya', in fact, meant preparing for independence whether or not the white man liked it.

Suddenly black African politicians were actually sitting at a table talking about forming the next government of Kenya.

The Europeans, bolstered over the years by promises from the British Government that they would rule Kenya for the rest of their lives, were aghast.

Only the most prescient of them, such as Michael Blundell, had been able to see it coming and had prepared to live and work within the new set-up. But who were these new African names that were coming to the top? How closely connected were they with Mau Mau? Would the dreaded Jomo Kenyatta return to power? What would these Africans do when they took over? Where would we go? These and many more were the thoughts of the European population who suddenly saw what they regarded as their country being snatched away from them.

Every utterance by a black Kenyan or British politician was closely studied to see how much there was between the lines. For the journalists on the *East African Standard* it called for considerable skill and understanding and for diplomacy and a lack of bias which might be deliberate or born out of ignorance, inexperience or insensitivity. It was not easy.

The man in the cockpit was Iain Macleod, the new Colonial Secretary, who took the post after a Tory landslide victory in the General Election of October 1959. He was expected to back the European population, which included his own brother who lived in Kenya.

But the Europeans were in for a rude shock. There were to be no words of comfort from the motherland. Iain Macleod was working profusely to fan the wind of change and to hell with any supposed promises that had been made to the white population.

In desperation we hung on to his every word and on to every word from the other political participants. I remember one journalistic colleague not long arrived from Scotland. He was struggling to make something of a press release and he shouted out to the newsroom, 'Who's this guy Iain Macleod anyway?' There was a stunned silence. We had but one thought: if that is the level of his knowledge how the hell can he compile a report which took full cognisance of the situation and showed an awareness of the various sensitivities that abounded?

Three mouths after I arrived back in Kenya the Belgians gave independence to the Congo and the whole place fell apart with an unleashed black population launching a reign of terror against the whites. The headlines were full of stories about massacres, cannibalism and the raping of nuns.

Many of the Belgians who were lucky enough to escape headed for Nairobi and I was assigned to interview some of them on their arrival.

There was plenty to choose from – three trains carrying more than 400 refugees arrived in Nairobi. One of the trains was met by no less a personage than Lady Renison, the wife of the Governor of Kenya. My report the next day stated:

> Eager hands grasped the luggage, strong arms took care of the babies and smiles of sympathy and understanding broke the language barrier. Cartons of hot coffee, milk, soft drinks and bars of chocolate were pushed into empty hands.
>
> Interpreters moved among the crowd, settling language difficulties. Without a hitch, the entire trainload was shepherded towards the exit, filtered out into cars provided by No 1 Round Table, Nairobi, and driven to the transit camp.

Many husbands and fathers had stayed behind in the Congo to look after property and to continue their way of life in the hope that their families would be able to rejoin them when the independence fervour had spent itself out. It was a forlorn hope. One of the interpreters told me, 'These people are still shocked at the quick change of events in the Congo. They had all heard people say it would happen, but somehow they just did not believe it.'

This carnage virtually on their doorstep as a result of Africans being given independence added to the fears of the whites in Kenya.

They thought it might be a useful political weapon in the talks with the British Government but the British Government was unswerving in its determination to hand over and get out as quickly as possible. Another factor undoubtedly overlooked at the time was that the circumstances in Kenya were not the same as those in the Belgian Congo. The Belgians have been widely and justifiably criticised for not preparing the Congo for independence, for not creating the necessary civil service groundwork and educational and social infrastructure.

Kenya was regarded as being different. Britain believed it had been a good colonialist and had trained the local population to the right level of competence to run their own affairs. The fact that the bulk of the local Europeans reckoned that the Africans were light years away from being able to run the country did not cut any ice.

The Africans, in fact, were more than ready, with many competent men queueing up to be given – perhaps, as some feared, even seize – the reins of power. The problem was that they had their deeply entrenched tribal hatreds and rivalries which could be stifled only in the meantime in a false show of unity while they grasped for the prize of independence.

But the fear was that the deep-seated tribal mistrust and acrimony would find their way back to a bloody surface – just as it now has after all those years since independence.

And looming in the background was the detained Jomo Kenyatta, regarded as the man behind the dreaded Mau Mau, which had perhaps precipitated the moves towards black rule in Kenya and maybe even in the rest of Africa.

There was no doubt that Africans of all tribes wanted him back and the political talks went ahead without the man who was obviously going to return as leader.

James Gichuru, the president of the Kenya African National Union, (KANU), the principal African party and undoubtedly the one which would eventually preside over the lowering of the British flag, returned on 31 October 1960 from a meeting in London with the Colonial Secretary and did his best to ease the tensions that were building up in his country.

He said that the country would be more at ease after the planned General Election in February. I asked him if he had raised with the Colonial Secretary the Kenyatta issue and he replied: 'How could you keep the Kenyatta issue out of it? I think the question is now so well advanced that it should be finalised here.'

Referring again to the upcoming elections, he stated: 'I hope the Europeans will be sensible and not return people who will antagonise the Africans.' So he had been conciliatory at the start of the interview and at the end of it had not helped European unease by advising them on how to vote.

Two weeks later Mr Gichuru was at it again. On the Sunday morning I had covered the Remembrance Day ceremony in Delamare Avenue, Nairobi, and when I had written my report the Chief Reporter, Eric Bales, told me I had to go to a KANU meeting at Naivasha, about an hour north of Nairobi, where the main speaker would be Mr Gichuru.

At these meetings African politicians usually spoke at length first of all in Swahili to the cheering thousands. Then they would give a brief summary in English 'for the benefit of the imperialist press' most of whom, of course, could not speak Swahili. This was because events in Kenya had attracted Fleet Street interest and the London journalists often went along to the political meetings to see what they could dig up.

In English during a five-hour meeting Mr Gichuru assured equal rights for people who accepted an African government after independence. Then he added in Swahili: 'We are no longer begging for *uhuru* (freedom) from the Europeans and Asians. They will soon have to kneel before us.' My Swahili was good enough for me to pick up that one and an African who was with me confirmed it. I had developed an unusual skill which was to be of considerable benefit in the coming years – to listen to a Swahili speech, translate it into English in my head and take it down in shorthand at the same time.

The result that particular day was a front page exclusive headed: 'They will have to kneel, says Mr Gichuru'. There followed an uproar which was heard as far away as London. Mr Gichuru claimed later that 'they will kneel' was actually a harmless Swahili idiom but nobody understood or believed him.

Nellie Grant, the mother of Elspeth Huxley, and legendary chronicler of Kenya history, writes in her book, *Nellie: Letters from Africa*: 'Terrific hoo-ha about Gichuru's speech at Naivasha in which he said the white man would after independence *piga magoti*, which means go down on his knees to the African. The press has said he ought to explain himself but he hasn't bothered. All pretty hopeless.'

There was another important development which added to the worries of the Europeans.

Peter Poole, a white man who shot dead a defenceless African, had been convicted and sentenced to hang. In many ways it was an open-and-shut case and there was no doubt about his guilt. But Poole would be the first European in Kenya to be executed for killing a black and this, at a time when tension between the races was high, made Europeans believe that he was destined to be

One for the family album - Irvin (holding bananas), Kelman (holding a lovely bunch of coconuts) and the author (holding a pawpaw and pineapple)

Rail wreckage by German troops in the First World War in Tanganyika, where Lt Paul von Lettow-Vorbeck pioneered guerrilla warfare

Ready to take on the journalistic world - white shirt, white shorts, long white stockings, black crepe-soled shoes, notebook

The African dhow in the Rufiji River, where Dow dined aboard a dhow

The author listens in to an interview with Louis Armstrong by the Kenya Broadcasting Corporation - it was his turn next to interview Satchmo

*The Land Freedom Army, an offshoot of what used to be Mau Mau,
still posed a security threat in the run-in to independence*

*Austin Reilly sits on the tortoise, a move which cures his bad back,
restores his golf prowess and attracts world attention*

One of the forty-five occasions when telephone wires
had to be raised to let the giraffes through

The author gets a lift from a Rift Valley farmer

All eyes are on Jomo Kenyatta as he gets a rapturous welcome in Nakuru after his release

The British Army was called in to help put down a mutiny after independence

a sacrificial lamb in this new and disturbing political game that was developing in Kenya.

The final word rested with the Governor, Sir Patrick Renison, a soft-spoken man who seemed out of his depth and had a look about him which indicated he wished he was somewhere else, who could grant him clemency. By this stage the Peter Poole case had become an event for the world's press. They were all there to cover the moves towards independence and they suddenly found this juicy little case on their plate.

White Kenya waited with bated breath to see what the Governor would do. On 12 August 1960, the Committee of the Council of Ministers met in Government House, Nairobi, to consider capital cases. There were nine of them round that table, including the Governor, and they had two cases on which to adjudicate.

One was Regina versus Anderea Lwango s/o Sahani and the minutes state: 'The Committee gave its advice, and the Governor directed that in this case the sentence of death should be commuted.'

The other was Regina versus Peter Harold Richard Poole, and the minute states: 'The Committee gave its advice, and the Governor confirmed the sentence in this case, and directed that the law should take its course.'

So that was it. The African who killed would stay in jail; the European who killed would hang.

That was how the European community saw it and the quiet Sir Patrick Renison became a villain overnight. Many regarded the Poole decision as his last chance to make peace with the European community, despite the overwhelming evidence against Poole.

So he was hanged and he was seen by the white community as no more than a scapegoat, a sop to the Africans to show that there was no favour or bias towards any race.

In fact Poole, murderer that he undoubtedly was, was a victim of the times: there was some doubt about his sanity and if his trial had taken place in a less politically sensitive time with the world spotlight elsewhere he might well have had his sentence commuted and ended up in a mental home.

Sir Patrick Renison then won some favour back from the European community by refusing to release Jomo Kenyatta from detention, saying that he was the recognised leader of the non-cooperation movement which organised Mau Mau, with its foul oathing and violent aims. Kenyatta, said Sir Patrick, was 'the leader to darkness and death'.

Undoubtedly that is how he was perceived by the European population, but he was a leader nonetheless, and he was the leader that the African people wanted to take them to independence. This was the view shared by the two African political parties, the Kenya African National Union (KANU) and the Kenya African Democratic Union (KADU), although at times there were gaps and doubts in that unanimity.

This was because Kenyatta, a member of the powerful Kikuyu tribe, was undoubtedly a KANU man and would lead KANU to power, while KADU represented the lesser tribes and any unanimity they showed meant no more than that they were prepared to accept Kenyatta as their leader even as a short-term measure to hasten the arrival of independence.

Tom Mboya, a fast-rising star on the African front already marked by many as the successor to Kenyatta although the fact that he was from the Luo tribe and not the dominant Kikuyu would work against him, sensed that KADU might be lukewarm to the return of Kenyatta.

At a political rally in Nairobi he told a cheering crowd of 25,000 that both parties should boycott the pending elections unless Kenyatta was released. He said KANU had already prepared a flag that would be hoisted in place of the Union Jack after independence. The meeting passed a resolution demanding Kenyatta's release. KANU was in the driving seat and KADU, which represented the smaller tribes, was having to follow reluctantly. There was no release; there was no boycott.

Another political rally was something of déjà vu for me – the main speaker was the New Kenya Party leader, Michael Blundell. He had represented my debut into the reporting world when I had covered for the Clive House magazine at the Prince of Wales School – founder, publisher, editor, distributor J Dow – a speech he made at the school.

This time I was wearing an *East African Standard* hat. The Saturday rally was at Nyeri, a 200-mile round trip from Nairobi. Mr Blundell was on the platform with another New Kenya Party candidate, with the elections about a month away, and they took a bit of a roasting from the local European community who were concerned about security.

Mr Blundell said it was to be expected that emotions would run high during the election but all would be well eventually. One man complained about an elderly lady in a post office queue being told by an African that he would get her after *uhuru*. I could not help thinking that they were all living in the past – this was not a rural England which would forever be.

This was post-Mau Mau Kenya, gearing itself up for African rule, and life for that elderly lady in the post office queue would change for ever.

But Michael Blundell was at his reassuring best. He replied: 'All I can say is that my eighty-four-year-old mother has just come out here to stay with me. We have no worry about the future in Kenya.'

Mr Blundell was a notoriously fast speaker, but my shorthand coped. I had a nice story for the Monday morning, and when I got back to Nairobi that Saturday afternoon I joined my parents and some friends for a coffee in the Mocha, a popular rendezvous.

When I returned to the car disaster had struck. I had not fully closed a window and an opportunist thief had made off with my suit jacket.

With it had gone my cheque book and my press pass, but to my horror I discovered that I had also lost an engraved fountain pen and propelling pencil which my friends had given me when I left Dar es Salaam.

But I knew there was something else. I stared at the empty seat in the car trying to think what it was. Then it dawned. The thief had also made off with my notebook – my shorthand recording of an important speech by Michael Blundell and his confrontation with worried settlers.

In the office the next day I wrote about 800 words entirely from memory and it was a page lead. If Michael Blundell was unhappy about its accuracy he kept quiet about it. But every time the News Editor's phone rang that Monday I tried to make myself scarce.

That Michael Blundell meeting was on the afternoon of Saturday, 21 January 1961 and I had another assignment that night. I had to borrow a jacket from a friend – my wardrobe was not that extensive – and find myself another notebook before heading out to the airport.

There I met Julius Nyerere, who was the Chief Minister of Tanganyika. I had first met him years ago when he was a student in Dar es Salaam and was being given a send-off by his colleagues as he left for Edinburgh University. I covered it for the *Tanganyika Standard*, but it was no big event – small time politician heads for the UK.

By the time we met again in Nairobi he was big time, quietly leading his country to independence. He was stopping off in Nairobi on his way to West Germany for talks with Federal Chancellor Herr Adenauer and other German leaders. He was keen to talk to the Germans about economic development and possible financial aid. He told me: 'We want to tell the Germans that there is such a place as Tanganyika. I doubt if they have heard of us.'

Quite a bit of irony there – the Germans had ruled Tanganyika earlier in the century and had even opened a First World War front there. I do not doubt Nyerere's grasp of history but this was no time to talk about a war and there were certainly plenty of Germans still around who knew all about Tanganyika.

I tried to get some quotes from him about the situation in Kenya but all he would say was, 'Disunity and strife do nobody any good.' I'd heard rumours that after independence he might seek to merge Tanganyika with Zanzibar on what would be a 'trial' federation. He refused to comment, but that is, in fact, what happened after Tanganyika achieved its independence and assumed the name of Tanzania.

That was not my last interview with Nyerere.

On 1 May that year (1961) Tanganyika achieved internal self-government, the stepping stone to independence on 28 December. This was a momentous event in colonial history. While Kenya was bickering, jostling, threatening and worrying about the way forward Nyerere was quietly going about taking his country to independence.

I was on night shift in Nairobi the night before Tanganyika achieved internal self-government and the Chief Reporter said to me something along these lines: 'You know – Tanganyika becomes self-governing tomorrow and we are not carrying much of a story on it. We really should be doing something.'

I said, 'Why don't I phone Nyerere and speak to him?'

'You'll never get to him but it is worth a try.'

I tried – and I got to him. I very much doubt if he remembered me but I was surprised on this Sunday night to find that after phoning Government House, giving my name and the purpose of my call I was put through to the man who, within a few hours, would be Tanganyika's first prime minister.

He seemed surprised when I asked him what celebrations were planned. 'What celebrations?' he said. 'Why, it will just be another normal day.' I pushed for more and asked how he felt on the eve of assuming Prime Ministership and he replied, 'I haven't the slightest feeling about it.'

So my front page story carried the headline in capital letters 'It Will Be Just a Normal Day'; perhaps in Tanganyika but there were no normal days in Kenya.

The campaign to free Kenyatta continued. Renison would not release him completely but he was allowed out of jail and held in detention in northern Kenya because he was regarded as a menace to society. Whether or not he was a menace this 'leader to darkness and death' was allowed to hold a press conference while still in detention and he was revealed as no revengeful firebrand but a moderate man who was looking forward to all races in Kenya living together in harmony. This was Nelson Mandela thirty years early.

It was clear that Kenyatta's days as an enforced political outcast were numbered. Sir Patrick Renison was going to have to eat his words, and on 14 August 1961, nine years after his arrest, Jomo Kenyatta was allowed to go home.

The *East African Standard* produced a special edition. I was on duty at five that morning helping to cover the story. It was about nine in the evening before I got home, my eyes just about popping out of my head with fatigue. But I had little doubt that I had been covering an event that was a momentous one in Kenya's history. It was unquestionably the end of an era and the beginning of a new one. The trouble was that the racial and personality mix was potentially explosive.

For me, the excitement was not confined to the political front.

The bouquet had worked. Lorna had answered my call. She arrived in Nairobi on 28 August 1960. The night before she landed in Kenya I wrote in my diary: 'We are both determined that together tomorrow means together for life.' I am glad to say I have been proved right.

Lorna stayed initially with a reporter, Bill Keddie from Galashiels in Scotland, and his wife at their house in Karen in the Ngong Hills outside Nairobi, named after Karen Blixen. Karen Blixen died two years later and her death merited only five paragraphs in the *East African Standard* under the heading 'She Gave Her Name to Karen'.

Lorna was not with the Keddies for long. She moved as a paying guest with another family. A few nights later the family Alsatian died and its body was dumped in a bucket outside Lorna's bedroom. That night she was kept awake by the hyenas fighting over the carcass.

A week later the old man of the house died. Lorna lay awake all night hoping that there would not be another hyena eating festival outside her bedroom window.

By then she was working in the *East African Standard* bookshop – I was surprised to find that I did have some influence – while we saved up to get married. She had also moved into a rented cottage with a woman she had befriended.

Why all this shifting around? A good question. This may have been the Swinging Sixties back in Britain but it was the early Sixties in Kenya and we had not learned to swing. Happy Valley was a long time ago. Besides, I was living with my parents. Nowadays we would just move in together. Kenya might well have pioneered promiscuity and the phrase 'Are you married or do you live in Kenya?' but in those early *East African Standard* days it was 'You'll wait until you are married because you live in Kenya'.

So we planned our lives ahead in a country that was never dull but fascinating and rapidly changing. Before the year's end, we were under the one roof. My parents rented a farmhouse, Lynton Farm, at Kiambu, eighteen miles outside of Nairobi, and there was plenty of spare accommodation. Single rooms, of course, as we planned for our wedding six months away.

We were married in May 1961, in St Andrew's Church in Nairobi, the church of David Steel's father – David, nicknamed Stainless, had been a pupil with me at the Prince of Wales School and years earlier I had been at the inaugural service in the church as a representative of the Prince of Wales School.

The reception was at Lynton Farm and we were given a great send-off before spending our first night as a married couple in the Norfolk Hotel, which had been the legendary watering hole at the turn of the century of big game hunters and the multifarious characters that descended on Kenya in the scramble for Africa.

The choice of the Norfolk for the first night of our honeymoon was not a random one and was not based on cost – had it been based on cost we would have gone elsewhere. But the Norfolk was something of a magnet for somebody interested in the history of Kenya as I was – and still am – and I wanted to stay in the Norfolk before an era ended and perhaps the Norfolk with it (the era has gone, but the Norfolk is still there).

The Norfolk had been the venue for the trial of Delves Broughton for the murder of Lord Erroll in the Happy Valley case which made headlines, several books and at least one film.

Elspeth Huxley has said that the Norfolk was the sort of place where in the middle of the night an Italian count or an Austrian baron would be thrown through the window on to your bed. I'm glad to say we had no uninvited guests that evening and the next day set off for our two-week honeymoon, which was spent in Mombasa, a 360-mile car drive on a road which was partly tarmac but mainly a bumpy, muddy or dusty track on which you had to keep your eyes open for crossing elephants.

On our return we had an overnight stop at Hunter's Lodge, owned by J A Hunter, one of the last of the old-time hunters, who could tell a few tales about the goings-on in the old days at the Norfolk and the characters who had supped and over-supped there.

The lodge had virtually been taken over by President Tito of Yugoslavia and his entourage who were on a hunting trip but Mr Hunter found room for us and he and his wife Hilda were happy to pose for a photograph with us.

Years earlier I had read his enthralling book, *Hunter*, and had marvelled at the story of the man from the south of Scotland who had made such an impact on the big game world of Kenya, first as a hunter with elephant, lion, rhino and leopard very much in his sights but latterly as an avid conservationist.

So it was back to the *East African Standard* to start married life and it was also back to Lynton Farm, Kiambu. We were honoured by being given the one bedroom – with two single beds which we pushed together each night and in the morning my mother dutifully separated them.

Lynton Farm was a lovely spot, but it was a bit isolated and we were not totally at ease in a country of gathering unrest. There were fifty yards in semi-darkness between the garage and the house and we always seemed to cover the ground quickly while claiming there was nothing to worry about.

One incident highlighted some of the tension. One Sunday night Lorna, my brother Irvin and I went to the cinema. The first eight miles of the road to Nairobi were a bumpy, single track. It was raining heavily and I was peering into the gloom when I saw what seemed to be a log straddled across the road.

There had been one or two incidents of this nature in Kenya – the motorist got out to clear the obstacle and was promptly attacked by a gang. I was not going to be caught that way, so I gritted my teeth, put the foot on the accelerator and our Volkswagen bounced over the obstacle.

We reported the incident to the police then went on to enjoy *Our Man in Havana*. The next day we learned to our horror that we had run over an African nightwatchman who, clad in a khaki overcoat and full of beer, had stretched out on the road.

My only consolation was that the police reckoned we were about the fourth or fifth car to hit him that night.

My parents no doubt had it in their minds that we would stay on at Lynton Farm as a married couple, being under their supervision in a strange land while saving a bob or two at the same time. Sorry, folks, it might be logical to you but that's no way to start married life – Lorna and I had other ideas.

All except one of the *East African Standard* reporters were based at the head office in Nairobi. The exception was the one stationed at Nakuru ninety miles to the north of Nairobi. From there the reporter covered a large part of Kenya and was virtually his own boss. He operated from a company flat but because it had a dual purpose the rent was reduced. A company flat in Nairobi cost £30 a month but this one in Nakuru was £10 a month.

When you consider that pay of about £90 went into our bank each month this saving on the rent was considerable. The good news was that the *Standard* man in Nakuru was giving it up to go to Canada. The job was tailor-made for us. The only snag was that I had to persuade the editor that I was the man for the job.

I applied for the coveted Nakuru post before our wedding and was given a strong hint that I would get it. But the editor waited until I came back from my honeymoon before confirming that the job was mine, although observing that at the age of twenty-three I was on the young side for such a responsible position.

The date for our journey up-country to take over as the *Standard* man in Nakuru was set for 8 July 1961. I felt we could not have been given a better start to our married life. Everything was perfect.

But life can sometimes give you a brutal reminder not to take anything for granted, not to assume that everything in the garden will always be lovely.

A month to the day after our wedding I had been on the night shift and Lorna had met me in town after some shopping – she'd bought some odds and ends for our first home in Nakuru – and as we drove home to Kiambu it was all we could talk about. We were staying with my parents in Kiambu while we patiently waited for the Nakuru job to kick in and as we took a corner I saw a single bright light heading for me. I thought it was a motorbike safely on my right hand side. In fact, it was a car with only one headlight on and it was in the middle of a single-track road. The result was a horrific, head-on car crash which could have taken both our lives. We both had a lucky escape – I had only a few bruises but I never saw my spectacles or bow tie again – and it was

Lorna who took the brunt of it. She was thrown through the windscreen. She was unconscious and covered in blood and when I saw her slumped down I thought I had become a young widower. I shouted her name at the pitch of my voice several times. She groaned. Police and other people appeared on the scene. With their help I managed to get her to the local dispensary. A doctor arrived and attended to her. I phoned home to get Mum and Dad to come out as quickly as possible. They hastily got into their car and were about to leave when my father had a sudden thought and said to Mum, 'Brandy, brandy – we'd better take some brandy.' Mum struggled out of the car and dashed back into the house. A minute later she appeared, clutching a bottle of brandy, and she got back into the car. Almost as soon as she sat down she was up again and before an aggravated James Dow Senior could ask why she dashed back into the house. He fumed and fretted and drummed his fingers on the steering wheel before Mum reappeared, clutching another bottle, and breathlessly sat again in the passenger seat. 'Where the hell have you been?'

'I had to get some ginger – Lorna likes ginger with her brandy.'

Lorna's injuries were fortunately mainly facial and she has kept the scars to prove it but she was very brave and I would not have been surprised if she had decided there and then that Africa was not her country after all. But she was made of sterner stuff and, besides, we had a great adventure lying in front of us in Nakuru.

Satchmo and the Monkey who nearly Made it to Hollywood[*]

One of the most sought after assignments while working as a reporter in the *East African Standard*'s Nairobi office was airport duty. Kenya and its capital were very much in the news and it was a must on the list of places to visit by celebrities. Hollywood, in particular, had rediscovered Africa, and Victor Mature, Robert Mitchum, William Holden. Curt Jurgens, Clark Gable, Ava Gardner and Carroll Baker were among those who landed at Embakasi Airport as it was then known and played host or hostess to the press – or tried their best to avoid them. The airport run meant, therefore, that you were given the opportunity to interview somebody famous, but we also got a shilling a mile expenses for using our own car, and a round trip to the airport meant twenty shillings on the expenses. Notch up a few of those in a month and you were doing well.

So there was a scramble for airport duty and I did not feel that I was getting enough of these lucrative airport trips to interview the big names. I have to admit that I did meet William Holden and Mary Pickford. I had a chat with Vic Oliver, Sir Winston Churchill's son-in-law. I interviewed the Archbishop of Canterbury Geoffrey Fisher, the Prime Minister of Southern Rhodesia Sir Edgar Whitehead, and the German film star Curt Jurgens.

Not bad, I suppose, but I seemed to be sent out to meet a lot of run-of-the-mill politicians and leaders of trade missions promising the earth to Kenya once the Africans were running the show. That was all grist to the mill, getting my stuff in the newspaper and adding to the expenses.

But I felt I was not getting my share of the action, so to speak, not meeting enough of the exciting visitors, but I eventually got my just reward.

---

[*] Darwin the monkey features on this cover of this book.

I drew the plum: Louis Armstrong.

He was on an African tour with his wife, his doctor, his valet, five musicians, his manager and, of course, his trumpet.

This was the beginning of the cola war which is still going on between Coca-Cola and Pepsi-Cola. Pepsi-Cola had hit the headlines by putting up $300,000 to send Satchmo on a promotional tour of Africa.

It was on the evening of Thursday, 3 November 1960 that he landed in the dusk at Nairobi. I had been grappling during the day with a story on the future of the Railway African Union and about a big contract which had been awarded by Nairobi City Council. But I saw during the day that nobody had yet been marked in the diary to cover Satchmo's arrival. Late afternoon I managed to persuade the Chief Reporter, Eric Bales, that I should cover the story.

So off I went to the airport along with a photographer to meet the great Satchmo (and, of course, to clock up another £1 on the expenses).

Needless to say, I was not the only one heading to the airport to meet the King of Jazz.

There was a Nairobi jazz band there to greet him with 'When You're Smiling' and 'Blueberry Hill' – I stressed in my report that it was a multiracial band because that was an important point to get across in those changing days.

A smiling Satchmo told the enthusiastic band from the airport balcony, 'That was swell boys. Maybe we can get together some time but right now I need some sleep and food.'

He had given about fifteen concerts in what was still the Belgian Congo, Ghana, Nigeria and Uganda, and I said to him that he looked tired. He laughed off this suggestion but his wife said, 'He is. It's not the work but all the travelling.'

The headline on my report the next day said: 'Tired Satchmo beams at jazz welcome.' My luck continued – Satchmo gave a press conference the next day and I was delegated to cover it. We were ushered into a lounge in the New Stanley Hotel where Satchmo stood waiting for us on a platform with his musical entourage. He introduced the various members of the band, adding 'he plays trombone' or 'he plays drums' and when he introduced his wife, Lucille, he said with his instantly recognisable mischievous grin, 'She plays with me.'

By this stage we were all seated, notebooks in hand, and Satchmo cast his eye over us, mopped his brow in his inimitable way and asked, 'Who's the dude who said I looked tired?' There was a copy of the *East African Standard* in front of him with my story on the front page.

There was no hiding place. Like a little boy in the classroom I meekly put up my hand and he pointed to his face and said: 'Don't you know that I always look like this?'

Then he gave us a summary of his tour so far, admitted that he had been a bit afraid in the Congo, then he asked if we had any questions.

Here was one of the best known black men in the world, the star of a press conference in the capital of an African country which was fighting for its independence. The neighbouring Congo was in turmoil – he had seen it for himself. The Europeans in Kenya still believed that the British Government was on their side. Kenyatta was still in prison and Africans were fighting for his release and for their country's independence.

There had been one or two instances where visiting American politicians had not hesitated to suggest that it was time the British got out of Kenya and that had sparked off rows. How dare they tell us how to run 'our' country? Anyway, how free are the blacks in America?

When Satchmo had arrived in Nairobi the previous night he had shaken hands with Tom Mboya, one of the KANU leaders, and he had heard a group of KANU supporters singing a freedom song. And the following evening he was to attend a KANU reception hosted by Mr Mboya.

So given those circumstances and that background – the fact that he had already made what some might interpret as at least one political gesture – it would have been quite legitimate to ask him for his views on the political situation in Kenya and on the struggle by his black brothers to win independence in Kenya and in other parts of Africa.

He looked at me, the dude who thought he looked tired, to ask the first question. And what deeply incisive question did this young, ambitious scribe come up with? 'How often do you buy a new trumpet?' Brilliant stuff, to be sure. (For the record, the answer was that he did not buy a new trumpet very often because he looked after his trumpet the way he looked after himself and gave it a good clean out once a week.)

In my defence I must point out that the questions from the other journalists were just as weak. Asked by another scribe how the African climate was affecting his playing he replied: 'I perspire a little when I blow but I never faint or anything like that because I'm cool all the time.'

The rest were in similar vein. It has to be said that at the outset Satchmo had told us to ask questions just about music. 'Don't talk about politics because I don't understand – the words are so big that by the time they're broken down to my size the joke's over.'

So it was all pretty light-hearted stuff. I can only think that the half dozen journalists – all of us pretty young – were really in awe of the man and did not want to try to stir up trouble by asking him political questions.

Why was he attending a KANU reception the following night? Was he endorsing KANU? Did he know that there was a rival KADU party? Did he have any views on the Kenyatta issue? I suspect that journalists of today, myself included, would not hesitate, but Satchmo cleverly remained apolitical and we did not have the nerve to disturb that.

My diary recording that day states: 'I saw him close at hand for long enough and even asked him how often he bought a new trumpet! What a character that man is – I really regarded today as a milestone in my career.'

I was not lucky enough to meet another Hollywood great who visited Nairobi but he tried very hard to take away with him a member of the Dow family.

That star was Edward G Robinson, but this story goes back many years to 1949 and back home in Carrick Knowe, Edinburgh. There was a German lady who was selling up and going back to Germany now that the war was over. My mother was one of those who went to her house to look at what was for sale. She did not have very much money so I doubt if she was going to buy anything anyway. It was no more than curiosity.

In the house an ornament caught her eye. It was a monkey sitting on a pile of books about Darwin's theory. The cross-legged monkey is holding a human skull in his hand and is gazing at it quizzically. Clearly, he is saying to himself, 'Is that how we end up?'

My mother asked the woman how much she was selling this eye-catching monkey for and was immediately told that it was not for sale. She clutched it to her bosom and said it had been in her family for many years and would be going back to Germany with her.

The next night there was a knock at the door. We were an upstairs house and by the time my mother got down to the door there was nobody there.

But on the doorstep wrapped in a blanket was the monkey, with a note from the lady stating that when she had completed the packing there was no room for the poor monkey. My mum was the only one who had shown an interest in him so she gave the prized monkey to her in the hope that she would look after him.

Look after him she – we all – did. He was soon christened simply 'Darwin' and that monkey with the puzzled look on his face has accompanied the Dow family back and forward to Africa for years.

He has become part of the family, and on my fortieth birthday my mother officially bequeathed Darwin to me.

He is still a complete mystery to us. A German friend of mine virtually froze in horror when he saw it in my house. This, he said, had all sorts of Nazi connotations. We are also told that Hitler had a Darwin in his study.

So the monkey with the mysterious background has become a member of the family, a constant eye-catcher and talking point.

In 1962 Edward G Robinson was in Kenya to make a film called *Sammy Going South*. It was well known that he was a keen collector of antiques and unusual ornaments and this was not lost on Bill Harris, a reporter on the rival *Daily Nation*.

Bill hailed from Fife and he was a close friend of the family.

He knew all about Darwin and he suggested to my father that he should contact Edward G Robinson to see what he thought of him.

Dad was reluctant.

Why would Edward G Robinson, this great Hollywood star, be interested in Darwin?

I think Dad envisaged nothing but embarrassment if he tried to go through with it. Not the bold Bill Harris. A compromise was reached – Dad would not be involved but Bill would seek out Edward G and introduce him to Darwin.

Edward G was staying at the New Stanley Hotel in Nairobi and it was not too difficult for a reporter to arrange an interview with him. Bill did just that and met him in the hotel, carrying Darwin wrapped up in a blanket. A brief conversation ensued and, in a scene which might well have gone down well in one of Edward G's movies, Bill whipped the blanket off Darwin after a careful look round the room.

Edward G stared wide-eyed at Darwin and said three words: 'Name your price.' He was determined to have Darwin at any cost but, of course, he was not Bill's to sell. So it was arranged to meet again, this time with my dad to accompany Bill and Darwin.

Dad was not going along to sell. A day earlier he might well have sold Darwin to Edward G for a modest sum and would have enjoyed telling the tale for years after. But when he found that Darwin might actually be worth a lot of money he became protective and decided to keep Darwin.

But he still wanted his meeting with Edward G and we were taking bets within the family as to whether the Hollywood star would smooth talk Dad into a deal.

Alas, we never found out. Edward G suffered a heart attack the next day and had to go back to America.

So Darwin stayed in the Dow household – the monkey who nearly made it to Hollywood.

THE MURDEROUS GANG ATTACK WHICH SHOCKED KENYA

David 'Scottie' Osborne and his wife, Nora, on the night of Friday, 5 May 1961, in their Mau Narok farm enjoyed their evening meal then both dozed off in front of the roaring fire. This was the Highlands of Kenya and it could get chilly at night.

Scottie had come through the Emergency and was always alert to the possible dangers in their remote farmhouse but the Emergency had been over for more than a year and he felt he could relax a little.

Two windows in the sitting room were slightly open. The next thing Scottie remembered was waking up on the floor about fourteen feet away. He could see the legs of about five men standing around him. His back was to the fireplace and he was unable to see where his wife was.

He tried to grab one man by the legs but he was beaten heavily on the head with what he thought was a club. As he fell to the ground head he received another blow which broke his false teeth. Just as he hit the floor he heard a yell from his wife.

He heard the drawers of his writing bureau being opened and things being thrown on the floor. He heard the gang moving about the house. A man returned to tie his hands with string but the string broke so they were tied with wire.

He heard the men talking in Kikuyu, a language with which he was very familiar. His pockets were searched as he lay on the floor, and a man put his hand underneath his jersey and felt his chest. Then he heard the men leave in what he assumed was his car and he crawled across the room to see how his wife was. She had, in fact, been beaten to death by a gang of six.

He managed to drag himself upstairs and was relieved to find that his three-month-old daughter and fifteen-month-old son were sound asleep in separate rooms and were unscathed. The telephone had been cut and he had to shout from the verandah several times before his cook came and untied him.

The attack on the Osborne farmhouse and the brutal murder of Nora Osborne sent a shudder of horror through the European community in Kenya.

It was the nightmare of the Emergency starting all over again and this at a time when Britain was preparing to hand over power to the Africans.

Elspeth Huxley's mother Nellie Grant was among the shocked. In her *Nellie: Letters from Africa* she states: 'It was, of course, a ghastly murder, but I cannot think why David Osborne, who was always in a flap about security [he had his mill and his house burnt down before by the Mau Mau] should have let himself go to sleep with an open door and no weapon. Everyone says the 1952 pattern is emerging daily – it isn't really a life.'

I sat throughout the trial of the accused men and there was no evidence which suggested that Scottie Osborne had left the door open. He had admitted that two windows in the sitting room were slightly open, but no more than that.

Covering this trial was my first assignment as the *East African Standard* staff reporter in Nakuru and it was certainly a harrowing experience.

Standing in the witness box while describing the events of that night on which his young wife was brutally slashed to death and he was badly beaten was undoubtedly a painful experience for Scottie Osborne. And he had to go through it no fewer than six times.

At that first trial in Nakuru four men were found guilty of the murder of Mrs Osborne and sentenced to death after ten days of evidence.

But there were two members of the gang still on the loose and the Nakuru police showed stolid determination in bringing them to justice. One more was sentenced to death two months later on 27 September and the final member of the gang received the same fate on 19 November.

That meant three trials and three preliminary inquiries to determine whether or not there should be a trial. Scottie Osborne braved his way through the evidence of all six of them, making 1961 unquestionably a year of ordeal for him.

Apart from my feeling of extreme pity for Scottie Osborne, my lasting impression of these trials, and in particular the first one when four men were in the dock, was the complete naivety of the accused men. Even though the evidence was translated into their own language they did not seem to understand what was going on and seemed to hold to the belief that even if they admitted being members of the gang if they could show that they did not actually hit Mrs Osborne they would be found innocent.

'I did not kill. My job was to break the door. If I had known there would be death I would not have gone.' That was what one of the accused said before he was sentenced to death, and that summed up the view of the gang.

The gang of six had planned the raid in Nakuru then made their way out to the Osborne house at Mau Narok and had spent the night in a hide on the edge of the forest, overlooking the house. After dark two members of the gang were sent to reconnoitre the farm. They reported that the Osbornes were dozing by the fire and the cook was out of the way. The gang then pounced.

One Saturday morning a year after the murder Lorna and I set off to Narok deep in Masai country to cover a political meeting being held by the Kenya African Democratic Union (KADU). On the way there I slowed down as we passed the Osborne house and pointed it out to Lorna.

The main speaker at the meeting was Ronald Ngala, the president of KADU (subsequently to die after independence in a mysterious car crash) and we sat listening to him in sweltering sunshine surrounded by ochre-covered elders and spear-carrying Masai *moran*. The message from the meeting was that the Masai intended to fight for their sacred land in the Kinangops, the heart of the White Highlands. What they meant was that once they got the Europeans out they would take over this fertile land and it would not go to the Kikuyu.

But it was all friendly enough and we enjoyed a picnic in the midst of these fine warriors.

At 4.45 we set off for Nakuru amid warnings that rain was on its way and that this could make driving tricky on the muddy road. But we had to get home. Forty-five minutes later we were hopelessly stuck in the mud. I got out to try to push the car free. There was no way I was going to allow my dear wife, three months pregnant, to help me push the car, but I did ask her to get out of the car and stand on the grass at the side of the road.

Only the crickets disturbed the gloomy silence of that African night as I took a deep breath and tried to free the car from the mud. No chance. I took a breather and peered around me. That is when to my horror I saw that we were marooned right next to the empty Osborne farmhouse. I could see the edge of the forest where the gang had laid up after consulting a witch doctor. Then I heard hushed voices in the darkness and realised that armed figures were slowly approaching us out of the African night. I looked at Lorna and tried not to appear frightened, hoping she had not realised how close we were to the Osborne farmhouse.

Then I recognised that we were being approached by a group of Masai tribesmen, carrying their spears and shields, offering to help us. I doubt if anybody has ever been so grateful to see a group of armed Masai in the middle of Africa. A few grunts and heaves and we were on our way.

Not for long. Further up the road we were stuck again. No Masai to the rescue this time – but a Land Rover bringing some of the speakers back from the KADU meeting we had attended. Out jumped Wafula Wabuge, the Member of the Legislative Council for Nakuru, and Martin Shikuku, General Secretary of KADU. They had no hesitation in helping – this time the Land Rover towed us out.

But I was obviously determined on a hat-trick because ten miles later I got stuck again. This time the rescuers were quite different – a bunch of Europeans returning from a wedding in Nakuru. They were all dressed in their finery and, as they say, drink had been taken, but this was Africa and the men soon had their shirts off and their evening trousers rolled up and were happy to gambol through the mud and push us clear. There was a festive air about it this time.

We had a clear run home after that, and we got back to base at around nine in a car which looked like a massive mobile mud pack. We were not in too clean a state either but I had a story from the meeting which made the front page.

Witchcraft had figured largely in the Osborne trial. A witch doctor had been consulted in advance about the raid and had produced a grimy, crumpled piece of paper on which there were strange markings. This, said the witch doctor, meant that only six members of the gang should go on the raid. A seventh was told that he would have to drop out – and he proved to be one of the main prosecution witnesses at the trials.

This was not the only time that the subject of witchcraft cropped up in my coverage of events in Kenya north of Nairobi. I reported then faithfully, not because of any fears of failing victim to a spell but because it was part of the news and if witchcraft set off a chain of events the duty was to report it and not scoff at it.

One of the players in the Molo Football League dropped down dead during a game. The result was that three of the teams in the thirteen-team league refused to kick a ball for a month because they were convinced that a witch doctor had intervened on behalf of one of the teams. To take the field they reckoned would mean certain death. It took a lot of wisdom and patience by local sports officials to sort than one out and get the players back on the pitch.

In another incident a woman accused her mother of using witchcraft to prevent her having a baby. She claimed that she had lost seven children through her mother's witchcraft but her husband had paid his mother-in-law a cow and a goat to persuade her to lift the spell and allow his wife to have a baby. She lifted the spell – and the wife had a baby.

But later the mother was caught in the act of performing a witchcraft spell and that was enough for the wife, who thought she must be up to no good again – so she killed her mother with a spear.

It was a cold-blooded murder based on something most people would laugh at and greet with hearty disbelief but it was to the credit of British justice, showing a degree of flexibility not always evident, that the judge agreed that witchcraft was a grave act of provocation and he sentenced the woman to one day in jail for killing her mother.

There was even a Witchcraft Ordinance. I never did understand it, but the implication throughout this piece of legislation was that witchcraft was regarded as being genuine enough – it was how it was used that was important.

In one case a witch doctor was asked to investigate a livestock theft. He invited more than 100 people to a tea party and set about trying to discover the culprit.

He gave everybody a cup of 'tea' and said it would make the thief feel ill. Nobody knows what he put into that brew but he made more than the thief feel ill – almost as soon as the 'tea' was down about twenty people became ill. Some fell to the ground in a trance, which in some cases lasted about fifteen hours. Others rushed around tearing their clothes off.

The sufferers were told that they would be given the antidote in return for the payment of one cow. They paid up and all of them recovered – except one guy, and he went to the police.

How did the police handle the outcome of this tea party? Under the Witchcraft Ordinance they were able to charge the witch doctor with pretending to exercise witchcraft, using witchcraft with intent to injure and attempting to solve a crime by the use of witchcraft.

I would have thought that the charge of pretending to exercise witchcraft would have ruled out the other two charges. The witch doctor pleaded guilty – how could he deny using witchcraft when that was his livelihood? A sympathetic magistrate gave him a light sentence. The livestock thief, by the way, was never identified.

Witchcraft incidents like this were part of everyday life out in the bush, far from what we would regard as civilisation, but sometimes witchcraft was much closer to home.

The Pyrethrum Board dealt with a crop which was an important part of Kenya's economy and it operated in Nakuru itself. It had to organise a witch doctor hunt in its factory along with the Kenya Chemical Workers Union to try to find the witch doctor who had cast a spell on a European and an African employee.

The trouble started when an overseer claimed he was sick and he was given seven days' sick leave. He later wrote to the senior supervisor, a European, saying that he had consulted his own witch doctor and been told that the culprit was a man at the factory who was disgruntled about being moved to another shift. He had then done something not in the trade union handbook: he called in a witch doctor to cast a spell on his boss.

However strange this might seem, it worked. The boss did become unwell and was too frightened to return to work. He contacted his own witch doctor but he could not lift the spell – that had to be done by the original witch doctor.

The European supervisor on whom a spell had also been cast had no ill effects. But he was not a believer – and even if he had acquired some malady as a result of a witch doctor's spell I doubt if he would have admitted it.

His main concern was to keep the factory operating smoothly and it was not doing so as long as the witch doctor was at large. The overseer never returned to work and the factory got back to normal.

Nobody suggested that witchcraft was a load of nonsense. It was part of African life, and you had to look out for it, whether it was on the football field or in the factory.

I Cross Swords with Jomo Kenyatta

In February 1961 the Committee for Racial Cooperation in Kenya published what it called 'Kenya 1961', which it described as a brief but accurate and objective summary of the situation in Kenya on the eve of elections to be held that year as an outcome of constitutional discussions convened at Lancaster House, London in February 1960.

The document was put together by Elspeth Huxley, the Kenyan writer, Charles Hobson, a former British Labour MP, Peter Remnant, a former Conservative MP, and Jeremy Thorpe, who was then the Liberal Member for North Devon.

What they had to say was as much an enlightening commentary on British politics from a cross-section of British Parliamentarians as it was a summary of the Kenya situation.

It said that the election campaign was now reaching its peak in Kenya and African leaders were being accused of extremism and inflammatory statements. It continued:

> However, it is worth remembering that election speeches containing rather wild, irresponsible and often improbable statements are made in the United Kingdom in efforts to secure votes.
>
> The same is probably true in Kenya, and it may well be equally true that after the elections are over responsible realism will tend to prevail again, where it has not recently.
>
> Generally speaking, Africans have not reacted to statements by some Europeans hardly likely to promote racial cooperation.
>
> It is probably fair to say that Africans are now very largely, if not wholly, concerned with securing African votes. Europeans have been concerned mainly with constituents of their own race who decided the primary elections but now have to appeal to African voters also; not, in many cases, an easy matter.
>
> Compared with elections in the United Kingdom a great difference in Kenya is that the electorate tends to believe what it is told. There is a great need for leaders of all races to face their own people with the facts. Mr Nyerere did this in Tanganyika.

If the African leaders do not do so in Kenya the security situation could deteriorate quickly, once it is realised that Independence is not due in March 1961.

(In fact, independence arrived in December 1963.)

The document went on to discuss the release of 'the Mau Mau leader Jomo Kenyatta'. That choice of words is worth a comment – Kenyatta never admitted being the leader of the Mau Mau and his conviction for leading the terrorist movement was always a touchy subject because it was felt that he had been found guilty for reasons of political expediency, with the legal case and evidence against him being extremely flimsy.

Nonetheless, the Kenya population as a whole had little doubt that he had one way or another been the leader of the dreaded Mau Mau. For the vast majority of Africans this was to his credit and was his political passport; for the white population it justified the governor, Sir Patrick Renison, describing him as the leader to darkness and death.

However, for the Committee for Racial Cooperation in Kenya, an organisation dedicated to racial cooperation, it was a bit of a risk to come out and state unequivocally that he had been the Mau Mau leader, and it might well have started the political furore it was seeking to avoid. However, the wayward words slipped by unnoticed in what was a torrent of pre-election words from many organisations and parties.

What the document undoubtedly highlighted was that great care had to be taken with what was said or written because the country was passing through an extremely difficult and potentially explosive stage.

We were facing a general election – the first of its kind in the country's history because this time round we were talking about nationwide suffrage. The winners would undoubtedly eventually lead an independent Kenya and there were bitter rivalries among the tribal factions fighting for power.

It would also be popular, vote-catching stuff to take a dig at the Europeans, who had been the imperialist bosses throughout the century and were at last being shown the door, even though the forward-thinking African politicians realised that those Europeans had a lot to offer an independent Kenya.

But the bulk of Europeans saw nothing but danger and isolation ahead, especially when the man the Africans regarded as their true leader, the supposed Mau Mau leader Jomo Kenyatta, was waiting patiently in the background.

The Kenya 1961 document summed it up this way:

> Her Majesty's Government has stated that so long as he is considered a risk to security in the opinion of the Governor he should remain in detention.
>
> Any decision other than to continue detention should, the Committee [for Racial Cooperation in Kenya] feels, be preceded by the most careful review of the situation in the light of all evidence available.
>
> The release of Kenyatta is a tremendously powerful emotional issue in Kenya now, and it seems likely to persist as such after the elections.

The elections were being fought by the two main African parties – the Kenya African National Union (KANU) and the Kenya African Democratic Union (KADU). Both of them had as their goal unity in the country in the final campaign for independence, but tribal fears and ambitions could not be papered over along with the fear that post-independence they could tear the country apart.

KANU was dominated by the country's two major tribes, the Kikuyu – of which Jomo Kenyatta was a member – and the Luo, and its leaders – James Gichuru, Tom Mboya and Oginga Odinga (father of Raila Odinga, whose confrontation with Mwai Kibaki for presidency has brought Kenya to the brink of civil war), all of whom I have interviewed – wanted a strong unitary constitution to bind the country together.

KADU, led by Ronald Ngala, Musinde Muliro and Daniel arap Moi (later to write his name large in Kenya's history as President), feared domination by the major tribes and favoured a federation of regions with specific powers. This was aimed at protecting the smaller tribes, and was known as 'regionalisation', the Swahili equivalent being *majimbo*.

It was complex political environment, bristling with dangers, especially for this young journalist attending political meetings every weekend in outlying parts of Kenya, standing in the midst of frenzied crowds, many carrying spears and shields, listening to impassioned politicians seeking their favour and condemning their opponents, black and white.

As I've already noted, most of the speeches were in Swahili, with either a public English summary given by the speaker at the end or a private interview later with the politician to be given his version of what he had said. Neither was really satisfactory – it was not competent journalism to ask a politician to tell you what he had said. You were there to report what you had heard him say in public. He was quite happy, talking to you privately afterwards, to give you a sanitised version, leaving out all the contentious material which had brought the crowd to its feet.

But if you singled out the inflammatory passages of a speech and highlighted them, because, after all, it was news, were you unnecessarily adding to the flames by using material which was just put in as a crowd-pleaser? There were some who took this view, and the journalist became the villain simply because he reported the message. I had already caused a bit of a furore by reporting that James Gichuru, the president of KANU, had told a meeting in Swahili that the Europeans would kneel after independence.

But it was not up to the journalist to act as a censor – the job was to report what the politicians said, and it was up to the politicians to choose their words carefully and to try to work out and anticipate the ramifications of the statements they made at political meetings.

For the journalist, it was a difficult path to tread, and I had obviously upset Mr Gichuru, who did not realise that there was a white, Swahili-speaking journalist in his midst. It was an experience that I was to repeat with the great man himself, the so-called leader to darkness and death, Jomo Kenyatta. He was eventually released from detention in August 1961 to the delight of KANU and KADU, who had been united in seeking his release. But Kenyatta was unable or unwilling to capitalise on this show of unity and he became leader of KANU, positioning it as an undoubted rival of KADU.

He led KANU in 1962 to the second constitutional

conference in London, presided over by Reginald Maudling, the Colonial Secretary, with KADU all the more determined to push for *majimbo* to protect some of the smaller powers at regional levels now that Kenyatta was firmly installed as leader of KANU, meaning that that party would rule an independent Kenya and so would he.

The agreement eventually reached included an element of regionalisation in the constitution but there seemed little doubt that when KANU was eventually at the helm it would not be ceding any powers to the regions and would remove any hint of *majimbo*.

Soon after returning to Kenya from the conference Mr Kenyatta spoke at a Sunday meeting in Nakuru. The night before riot police in Nakuru had been called out after a street battle between rival KANU and KADU gangs. But despite the tension on the streets the only trouble at the meeting was verbal.

Mr Kenyatta said that during the London conference Mr Maudling had described KADU as 'these silly people'. He added, 'The Colonial Secretary told me that if we called the Kenya provinces "regions" these "silly people" would rejoice.

'That is the truth.

'We have agreed in the Council of Ministers not to attack each other but we did not agree to tell lies. What I am saying is the truth.'

This was delivered by Mr Kenyatta in Swahili. I had an African interpreter with me as a back-up and I immediately realised the far-reaching implications of what Mr Kenyatta had said. He was virtually saying there was no chance of KADU getting any sort of regionalisation and that the Colonial Secretary, despite all the public pronouncements, was on his side.

When I phoned my story over there was consternation in the Nairobi office. The editor, Kenneth Bolton, was soon on the phone, checking out the quote. He asked me if I could verify it further. This I was able to do – I had pretty good connections with the Special Branch, who covered all these political meetings, and they gave me very unofficial confirmation of what Kenyatta had said.

The story was across two columns on the front page the next

day. 'Mr Maudling said "Kadu Are Silly".' KADU and the minority tribes were outraged. Mr Kenyatta was not pleased either. He issued a statement denying that he had said the Colonial Secretary had told him that KADU were 'silly people'.

> In fact, what I had said was that KADU had behaved in a silly manner at the London conference under the chairmanship of the Secretary of State, thereby delaying the independence. I did not refer to the Secretary of State in any other context.
>
> I hope this statement will put the records correct and remove Mr Maudling from the KANU–KADU political arguments.
>
> I would further like to impress upon the press not to be concerned only with what may appear to be controversial statements made at public meetings, but also to bring out the positive and constructive statements. There were a lot of positive and constructive statements made at the Nakuru meeting which the press ignored.

The story had appeared on the Monday morning, but it was the Wednesday morning before Mr Kenyatta issued his denial. The first I heard of it was an the radio – the Kenya Broadcasting Service saying that Kenyatta had denied saying Mr Maudling had described KADU as being silly people.

Soon the phone started to ring – and one of the callers was the worried editor. He questioned me closely again about the speech and my verifications of it; I told him that apart from myself I had confirmation from four other sources.

The next day the *East African Standard* carried Kenyatta's denial – and a leader on the subject. It was a brave, stout defence of this young journalist and if ever there was an occasion when a reputable editor put his head an the block at a tense time in a colonial country moving towards independence this was it.

The leader said there were two parts to Mr Kenyatta's personal statement about his speech last Sunday at Nakuru.

I will now quote in full, because this is, in effect, the editor saying that the African hero who was destined to become the country's first Prime Minister was a liar. All based on my evidence.

The leader went on:

> With the first [part] we must be honest and say we disagree; the second we completely accept.
>
> In reference to the policy of regionalism, Mr Kenyatta now says he told his Nakuru audience that KADU had behaved in a silly manner at the London conference under the chairmanship of the Secretary of State, thereby delaying independence. The intention of this was to remove Mr Maudling from the KANU–KADU argument.
>
> We very much regret we cannot accept Mr Kenyatta's rendering of what he said. He may have intended to say, he may believe he said, the words he now uses. What he actually said, according to our reporter, was the sentence as originally reported, allowing for the translation from Swahili into English. For example, he used the word *wapumbafu*, which was translated as 'silly people', whereas it could equally well mean 'stupid people'.
>
> When the report reached this office on Sunday its possible consequences on relationships with KADU were recognised and a check was immediately ordered. It was then established that our European (Swahili-speaking) reporter was accompanied by an African interpreter and the note was written down at the time. Subsequently, a comparison was made with another, independent source, also African, and the report was verified. Moreover, Africans leaving the meeting were heard discussing this very point.
>
> On the second part of Mr Kenyatta's statement there is no disagreement. He certainly did make positive and constructive statements which were omitted when compiling a brief report. Unfortunately, compression must always occur because a verbatim report of even one speaker, talking at an average of 120 words a minute for one hour, would run to 7,200 words – and that would fill seven solid columns of print.
>
> In compressing, reporters choose what they consider to have news value and it is here that opinions differ. We are glad to take this opportunity of acknowledging Mr Kenyatta's claim to have made constructive and reassuring statements, including tributes to the police and advice to Africans on taking land in the settlement schemes.

The day that strong editorial appeared was another busy one for incoming calls – mainly from friends who knew I was at the centre of it all and feared for my safety in the fraught circumstances. My parents motored ninety miles from Nairobi to express their concern, but I have to say there was never any hint of threat in my direction.

It was also reckoned that I would be high on the list the incoming African Government was preparing of undesirable Europeans who would be deported on Independence. Again, that did not happen, but this was all symptomatic of the unease and uncertainly among the different races in the country at that time.

It was also a stark reminder of the important role of the press and the difficult task of treading carefully between the responsible reporting of what is said by politicians and being unwittingly the cause of public concern and even unrest for performing that public duty.

The editor followed up his leader by sending a memo to all members of the editorial staff on the subject of reporting politics.

He said that if other media concentrated on the controversial and the sensational there was no reason why the *Standard* should follow suit in reporting political speeches. All due weight should be given to constructive proposals put forward by speakers.

If there was some important controversial statement, let it be given in its context but not exaggerated in any way. Subeditors should be particularly careful to highlight the constructive parts of speeches, and the Chief Subeditor would endeavour to make sufficient space available to accommodate reports of political speeches which concentrated on developments and the economic future.

He went on:

> There is nothing in this injunction to restrain reporters and subeditors from giving the news in a report, but I do not wish to have sensational treatment of items which can only exacerbate the present difficult situation. We have an immense responsibility in trying to preserve political understanding and have enjoyed a good reputation in the past for our objectivity and impartiality.

He finished by stating that he was sending a copy of this directive to the Presidents of KADU and KANU in order to keep them informed of the newspaper's policy.

In a separate note to me he said he had issued the directive 'as we are getting greatly concerned over the critical attitude of politicians of all parties.' He said we should dwell upon the constructive proposals made by political speakers and rid ourselves of the attitude of mind which was receptive to their more controversial or threatening remarks.

It seemed to me that the editor, having made his public stand against Kenyatta, had decided that this show of strength was enough and that from now on the *Standard* would adopt a different approach. The journalists on the paper saw this as a policy of printing nothing which might inflame KANU–KADU passions.

Nothing from political meetings would be reported unless it was 'constructive'.

The fact that he had sent a copy of this directive to the leaders of KANU and KADU was particularly galling. It was as if he was saying to them, 'Go ahead and say what you like at political meetings – we will report only the constructive bits.'

This was wrong. It was what was said at these frenzied political rallies which was liable to increase the tension between KANU and KADU – not the fact that it was in the newspaper the next day. The knowledge that an alert journalist – possibly a Swahili speaker or perhaps accompanied by one – could be in attendance would act as a check against any political leader saying something that would incite the mob, anger his opponents or put the fear of death into members of other races.

The leading Kenya newspaper undoubtedly had an important role to play at this crucial stage in the country's history but the way to do it was not to act as a self-censor and give carte blanche to the squabbling country's leaders to say what they liked without fear of publicity and public recrimination.

The directive was a genuine attempt by the editor to cool down the situation and it seemed to work, despite misgivings among journalists about not being allowed to perform their role properly in reporting what the politicians were saying at these packed, frenzied political gatherings.

I was not looking forward to hearing outrageous statements at the next political rally and having to keep them well down the story while looking for something which could come under the heading of 'constructive' and leading the story with that.

In fact, it seldom happened. Other reporters might have had different experiences but a lot of the controversy disappeared. Sending the party leaders a copy of the directive had been a masterstroke because it seemed to make them realise that they did not have to make outrageous statements to get the headlines. All they had to do was to be sensible and constructive – and, in the view of the thousands who turned up to be turned on – a bit dull and unexciting and they would get good coverage.

It was over two months before Mr Kenyatta came into my area again – this time at Kericho, 100 miles away from our home in Nakuru. It was what we called the tea town – it was in the middle of Kenya's tea estates and Brooke Bond owned the local hotel, which was the height of luxury in the middle of lush greenery.

Greenery such as this, always a welcome sight, was unusual in Kenya, and Kericho had the monopoly on it because the skies somehow ensured that it had a heavy, regular and reliable rainfall.

It rained every afternoon at four on the dot. You could sit in the comfortable hotel by a roaring fire and as four o'clock chimed you would hear the first pitter-patter of the rain while the waiter wheeled in the afternoon tea trolley.

But I digress. Lorna was left to enjoy this decadence while I headed off to cover the Kenyatta rally. As well as being in tea territory Kericho was in the heart of rival KADU land. Security precautions at this meeting were stringent – the KANU youth wing was out in force and searching everyone who entered the stadium for 'dangerous weapons'.

I stood on my dignity and refused to be searched – I reckoned my pen was my most dangerous weapon and I told them that if they did not allow me in without an insulting search the words of Kenyatta would not be reported.

Given the furore the last time I had reported Mr Kenyatta I might have been taking a chance and, in retrospect, was being unnecessarily stubborn. Somebody was sent away to do a spot of consulting and after about ten minutes the word came back that I was to be trusted and did not have to be searched. Honour satisfied.

Mr Kenyatta, in the stronghold of his KADU opponents, was

diplomacy personified. He said that what he wanted was unity not only in Kenya but throughout Africa. There should be no tribal or racial discrimination in the new Kenya. It was a conciliatory speech in the stronghold of his political enemies – was the edict from the editor which was directed at the journalists actually having an effect on the politicians?

It might have helped tone down some of the speeches but it did not slacken the war which was building up between politicians and the press, the former feeling that they were unable to get their message across because they had to rely on a biased press and the latter starting to feel beleaguered in a country which would soon be ruled by the very people with whom they were crossing swords.

The Legislative Council was the venue for the next skirmish, with the newspapers and local radio – the Kenya Broadcasting Corporation – accused by some African politicians of 'twisting the news'.

Time for another *East African Standard* editorial.

> Despite all the rancour on the part of politicians over the ages, for there has been an immemorial war between politicians and journalists so Kenya need not think its tiffs are anything very special, they have a lot in common.
>
> They belong to just about the only two professions in the world for which long academic training is unnecessary. The difference is that, whereas in the hard school of newspaper life the inefficients go to the wall, politicians carry on.

But the chasing of headlines continued without any attempt to be constructive. I attended a political meeting in Molo, north of Nakuru, where one of the speakers was Tom Mboya, one of KANU's leading politicians.

There was a surprisingly small crowd and I wondered if Mboya would bother turning up. He did – and he launched into a tirade claiming that the British were trying to whip up trouble in Kenya, bribing people to take oaths and to make guns.

By making Africans fight among themselves the British would claim that the Africans were not ready for independence. What these British could do, he claimed, was to bring about another Emergency in Kenya.

It was emotive stuff to raise the spectre of another Emergency and to talk about oaths – it was the degrading oath-taking ceremonies that Mau Mau recruits had to go through, swearing to kill their enemies no matter the cost.

It did not help that there were already oath-taking ceremonies taking place in the Rift Valley and in particular in the Molo area where Mboya was speaking. I was reporting daily court appearances by people admitting to being members of what was called the Land Freedom Army – four days after Mboya's speech a Molo magistrate imposed jail sentences totalling 156 years on forty-five people who admitted being members of the Kenya Land Freedom Army.

One man admitted making thirty-eight guns; another was an oath-administrator who admitted administering oaths to more than 200 people in the Nakuru district. He had already spent some time in jail for Mau Mau activities, so Mboya was hitting a raw nerve when he spoke about the Emergency and oath-taking, but he did not back away from these statements and did not claim that he had been misreported.

My report was the subject of a heated debate the next day in the Legislative Council, the country's Parliament. Mr Mboya was by then Minister of Labour in a Kenya which was moving towards internal self-government, and it was stated in the Legislative Council that his Molo allegations were being investigated by the Government.

The fact that the announcement about this investigation was made by the Temporary Minister for Internal Security, Mr Ellerton, (for some reason on the *Standard* we never gave the first names or initials of Government ministers) carried with it the implication that it was not so much the allegations that were being investigated but Mr Mboya himself for making them and causing some concern among the populace.

Mr Mboya did not retract any of his Molo speech and, in fact, handed Mr Ellerton a letter repeating the allegations. He made the point that he was making the allegations as general secretary of KANU and not as a Government minister and he repeated his claim that there were strong allegations that the police and Europeans were implicated in the Land Freedom Army or in gunrunning.

He found support from Mr Kenyatta, who by now rejoiced in the title of Minister for Constitutional Affairs and Economic Planning. He told the house that he had been in the Rift Valley and the rumours and allegations were very strong.

Another leading KANU official, Vice-president Oginga Odinga, claimed that the Land Freedom Army was being financed by KADU and Europeans.

It was, in retrospect, almost good fun were it not so serious and worrying for people of all races determined to get on with their lives and preparing to try to live together in racial harmony in a country which had independence clearly in its sights.

Why should KADU be behind the Land Freedom Army when it was clearly a Kikuyu organisation, perceived as being a weak but potentially dangerous offshoot of Mau Mau? Why would the Europeans support the Land Freedom Army when it had clearly stated that its aim was to run the Europeans out of the country?

To be honest, I do not think there was enough journalistic investigation of what the Kenya Land Freedom Army was all about and that is as much my fault as anybody else's. This was an apparently treacherous organisation in an area I was responsible for covering and all I did was to report on the procession of people going through the courts without trying to find out more about the movement and its aims.

You could put it down to lack of experience on my part – or maybe I was just too busy to do in-depth pieces. The movement did not have any apparent spokesmen so they were not knocking at the publicity door and the Freedom Army never became a serious threat – it provided a lot of work for the police, provided a lot of copy for me and, I suspect, provided a lot of headaches for the likes of Kenyatta and Mboya who did not need a burgeoning terrorist movement when the country was moving to independence anyway. It was far better to blame this irritant on the political opposition and the Europeans.

In August 1963 Kenyatta, who in June had taken over as Prime Minister in a Kenya with internal self-government and full independence only a few months away, made several speeches in my area. He was becoming more statesmanlike by the day.

One memorable tour was of the Western Region, which

borders on Uganda. This was very much in KADU territory and Kenyatta was going his best to mend fences. If there was to be any trouble about the lack of regionalisation (majimbo) after independence this was a powerful region which could cause trouble and be difficult to police.

Regionalisation, in fact, was in the constitution, with six regions retaining considerable powers. But the fear in the minds of KADU, now the official opposition, was that come independence regionalisation would be unceremoniously ditched and the power concentrated in Nairobi where the large tribes of Kikuyu and Luo dominated. KANU, on the other hand, was worried about the regions getting too powerful and breaking away.

Covering this trip meant an overnight stay at the Rock Hotel just into Uganda at Tororo. It was a pretty full hotel and I doubt if so many African leaders and future leaders have ever been under the one roof.

Kenyatta and his entourage had booked in. Also staying in the hotel were Julius Nyerere from Tanganyika, Milton Obote from Uganda, Kenneth Kaunda from Northern Rhodesia and Joshua Nkomo from Southern Rhodesia. Nkomo, as it turned out, was the only one not to become leader of his own country but in those days I would have put money on him making it.

Some of them also attended Kenyatta's meetings the next day, and the message he was spreading on this extensive tour was of forgetting the past, eradicating thieving and working to build a new Kenya.

I interviewed him on the third day of the tour and found him looking fit and well after travelling more than 600 miles by car in two days and addressing several meetings. This was, in fact, my first interview with him – I'd been alongside him at many political meetings, taking copious notes, and he must have known that I was the cause of his public spat with the editor of the *Standard* which saw him, in effect, being branded a liar. But he did nothing but respond courteously to my questions, superbly playing the role of a smiling, wise old man. He reckoned his tour of the Western Region had been very successful and he could see no signs of moves towards autonomy.

This was the first time I had heard him use that word in connection with regionalisation. He was obviously taking it very seriously and it would remain part of the political debate for some time to come.

He certainly felt his Western Region trip had done a lot to help the unity process and he had shown some courage in meeting his political opponents head on.

But in that same month he had to tackle another powerful group – the white settlers, the farmers who had made Kenya what it was.

THE FUTURE PRESIDENT AS BABYSITTER

The Kenyatta focus had to be on Nakuru, which was virtually the agricultural capital of Kenya. It had been established by the British as part of the White Highlands and was Kenya's fourth largest city – and it was in Nakuru that Kenyatta was to make his historic speech that built many bridges between himself and the doubting farmers. It was a town in which Lorna and I quickly settled and it had a social life all of its own.

The hub for many was the Rift Valley Club and I should have been a member; it would have been an ideal place for meeting the right people and picking up stories, but I have never been a club person and have always been happy enough to make my own contacts. Professionally it might have been prudent to seek membership of the club but socially it was not necessary.

Nakuru had a pretty good rugby team – the strong South African population made sure of that – an excellent golf course and polo was enjoyed on the outskirts at Njoro, which was also the home of an agricultural centre now the Egerton University. Nakuru also had a football team, the Rift Valley Strollers, coached by a dedicated athlete who years later would coach the Swaziland team at the Commonwealth Games in Edinburgh and pay us a visit with half the team. I had one or two kick-abouts with the Strollers but even in those early days of my youth I was not as fit as I used to be.

Perhaps it was something to do with the lifestyle of Nakuru. Anybody who arrived in Nakuru would soon find invitations to dinner. It might be a couple you met only twenty-four hours earlier but the immediate move was to fix a dinner date at your house and entertain them. It was a constantly moving feast and in that social atmosphere Lorna and I had no difficulty in settling in while observing the social niceties of a town which was dominated by the colour pink. These were the flamingos on Lake Nakuru, the soda lake destined to become Lake Nakuru National

Park, and in getting into my car each morning there was always a quick glance at the horizon to check on the pink to establish that, reassuringly, the flamingos were still there. If the pink was fading I would contact the experts in case there was a problem because the Nakuru flamingos were always news. Occasionally we would pay a visit on foot to get a closer look at the flamingos but this could be a wee bit tricky because there were also hippopotamuses there and they did not always take too kindly to intruders or unexpected arrivals.

One anything but unexpected arrival – a bit on the late side – increased the size of the Jim and Lorna Dow family by one third. Karen arrived in the Nakuru War Memorial Hospital, a hefty wee soul weighing in at eight and a half pounds. We called her Karen after the suburb in Nairobi where Lorna first stayed when she arrived in Africa – it was named after Karen Blixen who lived there (later to be played by Meryl Streep in *Out of Africa*).

Our Karen made her first 'I'm on my way' moves around 10 on the Sunday morning and it was around 3.30 the next morning before she made her world stage debut, aided by a set of forceps wielded by the local Scottish doctor who knew a thing or two about babies – his wife resigned from the local family planning association after she gave birth to number six.

I had been up most of the Sunday night with friends supping beers and phoning the hospital – it's tough becoming a father for the first time – and I was able to see my tired wife and my two-hour-old daughter before I headed home for what was intended to be a sleep lasting at least until the morning.

But let us not forget that this young father was the local reporter, the scribe supposedly ready at the drop of a piece of copy paper to eagerly dash off to cover a red hot story.

My head had barely hit the pillow when the phone rang. It was the office in Nairobi. A couple from Bahati, about half an hour away from Nakuru, had been murdered by bandits while on holiday in Sardinia. I was told to visit the family home to get background details of the unfortunate couple and, if possible, a photograph.

'I've been up all night – I'm shattered.'

'Too bad – we can't send anybody from here.'

'But I've just become a father.'

'Congratulations – now bugger off to Bahati.'

'But I've had rather a lot to drink – I can't drive.' ('Pissed was not yet the vogue word in those days.)

'It's never stopped you before.'

He was right. In fact, it did not seem to stop anybody in Kenya, but that is another story.

So I set off for Bahati. It took me all of the afternoon and most of the evening to find the home and the bereaved family of the tragic couple and I got the necessary information and the photograph. My car got stuck in the mud on the way back but I managed to push it out – definitely a demanding task in the heat of the African sun for somebody suffering from an afternoon hangover.

Karen was born into a world of adventure she would never remember. She proved to be a good traveller – which was essential, because as a twosome Lorna and I had travelled a lot together and as a threesome my plan was to do the same.

It was nothing for me to motor four or five hours to cover a story and if I had to stay overnight the profit I made on the shilling a mile expenses more than covered the difference between a single room and a double room. Nearly a year after Karen was born we went on our first holiday. We had an overnight stop at my parents in Nairobi then drove to the coast at Mombasa, about 340 miles away, with a break halfway at Mac's Inn which was always popular.

The dark green Mini-Traveller was packed to the rooftop but we still managed to find room for the Moses basket that we had made specially for transporting Karen.

I recorded that day in detail in the hope that some day Karen would read it – or have it read to her – and wonder at it all. Perhaps the passage of time and the general familiarity with things African as a result of the television screen have taken the edge off any wonderment but for me it still evokes the magic of it all so that on reading it I can almost get the whiff of the African dust in my nostrils and the sense of excitement at driving down that long and tricky road in the cramped wee car with Lorna beside me and that little bundle somewhere among the luggage in the back.

Woke at 3.30 a.m. and we immediately got up. A cup of coffee and some toast and we were off at 4 a.m. as scheduled. Karen was restless for the first hour but settled down.

We thought we saw a hyena, then a lovely view of a leopard at the side of the road. Then impala, wildebeest, giraffe, zebra and, well into the afternoon, an elephant.

We got to Mac's Inn at 8.15, after an easy journey, although the road at times was very bumpy and stony. A welcome breakfast for the three of us and we set off at 9 a.m. The road thereafter was very easy, but terribly dusty. We got to the Shanzu Hotel at 1, just in time for lunch. Then on to the beach, with Karen really enjoying her first paddle in the sea. But the rooms are really wee – we can't find anywhere to put anything. But we're on leave and lapping up every minute of it.

While there I popped in to see the editor of the *Mombasa Times*, Ted Stairs, one of those who had taken me under their wing in my debut days on the *Tanganyika Standard* in Dar es Salaam and he offered me a job. He said he would keep it open for a few months.

I was flattered that Ted thought enough of how I had turned out to offer me a job and living on the coast undoubtedly had its attractions but by the end of the holiday I had decided to see out my time in Nakuru.

Karen's travels in the back of the Mini-Traveller in the comfort of the Moses basket started about a month after she was born. When she was old enough to sit in a car seat we fed her in it on the murram roadside. This was often while I was on my way to cover a political meeting and the friendly Masai and Sumburu warriors in tribal outfits would shout '*Jambo memsahib*' at Karen as they trotted by.

It was not always friendly. On one occasion I dropped Lorna and Karen off at the Wagon Wheel Hotel in Eldoret then went to an open-air political meeting at a place called Kakamega. My diary records: 'They were quite virulent in their attacks on Europeans and it was not very nice to be the only white face in the middle of the hissing mob.'

The afternoon meeting was just as bad and became quite unruly. Kenyatta's car was stoned and my vehicle suffered the same fate. The police had to use tear gas to break up some of the scuffles. This, to me, was 'all good stuff', and when I got back to the hotel Lorna and Karen greeted me as though I had just completed another quiet day at the office.

It was not only political meetings which took us on our travels throughout Kenya. A lot of my work involved court cases – if the story was big enough I would travel to the court and stay the night if necessary.

If I could not make it, the police prosecutor would give me the details on the phone and I would even phone the magistrate in his hotel at night and ask him what he had said in passing sentence.

Some trials would go on for days. Evidence was slow to get through, mainly because it normally had to be given in two languages, English and Swahili or Kikuyu. Sometimes the three languages were used – if the accused demanded that the evidence be translated into his own tribal language it had to be done.

One memorable case I covered in Eldoret concerned no fewer than thirty-seven men who faced charges in connection with political fighting which had followed a visit to the town of the Colonial Secretary.

The accused crammed into the dock and the long process started of reading out the charges and finding out which language each accused preferred.

It was bonus time for interpreters – five of them sat round a table as the evidence was read in English, Swahili, Kikuyu, Kamba, Maragali and Luo. I doubt if there is such a category in the Guinness Book of Records but if they created one for the most languages used in the one court hearing it would be this one in Eldoret, with six languages involved.

I stayed with it long enough to get the story about multilingual justice trying to operate in a remote part of Kenya but I'm afraid I did not have the time or the patience to see this one through to the end. Then there was the case of the Kericho candleman.

While Lorna and Karen enjoyed the comfort of the Kericho tea hotel I covered a murder trial which featured an astute bit of detective work.

The victim was an elderly South African woman and the accused was a local Kisii tribesman. The victim, a governess, had been strangled and the time of death was reckoned to be between

11 p.m. and 4 a.m. when the generator to the farmhouse was switched off.

It was essential for the prosecution to show that this was no panic attack and that the accused had not dashed off after committing the crime when the lights were out but had stayed on and looked around for valuables. The police had found an estimated sixty drops of candle wax in the room where the body was found, on the verandah and on the body itself. The Assistant Superintendent of the CID said he had carried out an experiment and found out that it takes one minute and ten seconds for sixty-two drops of wax to fall from a candle. That, of course, is if the candle is held at an angle of 45 degrees.

In the witness box with great panache the Assistant Superintendent reached into his briefcase and produced a candle. Then, as the hushed court looked on in what was a dim room, he lit the candle and proceeded to explain his newly discovered laws of candle dropping: 'If the candle is held upright in still air the grease evaporates and therefore it does not fall to the ground.

'If there is a current of air and the candle is held at an angle the grease drops.' He tipped the candle over to an angle of 45 degrees and the drips slowly fell to the courtroom floor. This sort of inspirational stuff which would have been comfortable in the Sherlock Holmes handbook was pretty rare in the Kenya courts and created more than a little interest and fame for the star performer but this was a murder trial and the candle wax evidence was important enough to send a man to the gallows.

But soon the courts started to fill up with people charged with being members of the banned Kenya Land Freedom Army, taking illegal oaths and the unlawful possession of home-made weapons. It made for a busy news schedule but it also made European farmers uneasy about the security situation.

That was when the story focus switched to the European farmers who decided to get out. There was no doubt that in many cases they were fleeing the country for none other than racist reasons – they could not live under a black Government at any price.

For many it was a genuine security worry and the apparent growing threat of the Kenya Land Freedom Army loomed large in their minds and brought back memories of the bad old Mau Mau days. I attended a lengthy meeting of a group of farmers chaired by a farmer who had been a Kenya Cabinet minister in the days before independence, and their statement afterwards said:

> The Land Freedom Army is relying on Kikuyu employees on farms and in the forests for support and information and supplies, so following exactly the system of the Mau Mau.
> Furthermore, in view of the widespread oathing ceremonies in our area it is probable that many men working on farms have been enrolled in a territorial force which will enable the regular Land Freedom Army to be expanded several-fold when required with the objective, as the Minister for Defence has stated, the seizing of Rift Valley farms after independence through a process of civil war.
> We are fed up and will not be messed about any longer.

Fed up they might well have been, but they really had only two options – sticking it out or getting out. For the man regarded as the firebrand of Kenya farming, Major L B (Jim) Hughes, it was too much. He decided to get out, and I went along, camera in hand, to his Kinangop farm to see it all go under the hammer.

I was not alone – his reputation for having the most up-to-date and efficient farming machinery attracted more than 100 buyers from all over Kenya, Uganda and Tanganyika. It was snapped up for what my report described as 'prices that were considered fair in view of the current market situation'.

The farm of more than 500 acres was bought by the Government as part of a land settlement scheme – giving it back to the Africans. The departing statement from Jim Hughes read: 'Twenty-four years of my life have gone in a few hours.'

As he posed with his Ayrshires, reckoned to be one of the best commercial herds in the country, he announced that he was going to South Africa. It was all done with a smile – no bitterness, as though he accepted that he had had his day and was now willing to move on.

For others it was not that easy.

To be sure, the Government was prepared to buy farmers out because they wanted to return the land to the Africans. But, inevitably, there were cries that the money being offered was not enough.

One story I wrote typified the situation and tragedy faced by many.

> To Morris Johnstone, an ex-RAF pilot who had settled to farm in Kenya, the letter from the Agricultural Settlement Trust seemed the end.
>
> The money he was offered for his land was not enough. He had had three bad years, and the future seemed bleak. He made one final visit to the Trust offices in Nakuru in an attempt to get a better offer, but it was in vain.
>
> That night Morris, who coached Army glider pilots before Arnhem, took his life, while farmers' representatives in London battled with the British Government for more money to rescue Kenya farmers from their plight.
>
> Officials of the European Association of Agricultural Settlement Board Farmers this week glumly heard the reasons for Morris's death and they are investigating a report that a second member has taken his life for the same reasons.
>
> The chairman of the Association, Wing Commander G A Saunders, who was a close friend of Morris, said: 'It is not too difficult to resettle if you are under forty, but if you are over that you cannot go anywhere else unless you have exceptional qualities.
>
> 'Many of our members have worked hard since they came out here and have spent a lot of money. Now the money they are being offered is ridiculous.'
>
> In a letter to Wing Commander Saunders his widow wrote: 'Morris became so discouraged over the last three years. The final straw was the price offered for the farm. It was not enough to start again. I will stay here for a while as at the moment I can't think...'

It was inevitable and righteous that Kenya should be given its independence and be returned to the Africans. But it was also inevitable that there would be many victims of this progress and Morris Johnstone was one of them.

He had hoped to be able to stay an in Kenya but the wind of change had other plans for him.

There were many transactions where the white farmer was

only too glad to take his money and get out. He usually went with insults being hurled at him by his ex-neighbours and friends if he was the first one to break the circle and allow a black farmer into the area. But they were pushing water uphill if they thought they could stop the political progress that was being made as Jomo Kenyatta moved towards becoming the first president of an independent Kenya and was developing into a statesman at the same time.

Meanwhile, the man who was to succeed Kenyatta as the second president, Daniel arap Moi, had other things on his mind. He was head of the Rift Valley Regional Assembly, which was headquartered in Nakuru and was the bastion of the *majimbo* (regionalisation) policy pushed by KADU to protect the smaller tribes and give them a measure of autonomy away from Nairobi. Moi was the *majimbo* leader. When he eventually became president *majimbo* was taboo because he wanted all the power to be in Nairobi and he was not too happy with any reminders of the days long past when he had espoused it. But when he was building his power base as head of the Rift Valley Regional Assembly anything the Assembly decided – usually cocking a snoot at the Government in Nairobi – he expected to be in the *East African Standard* the next day.

And that meant, as far as he was concerned, that the *Standard* staff reporter in Nakuru had to be in attendance at Assembly meetings, notebook in hand, no matter the circumstances.

One morning I was looking after Karen because Lorna was in hospital (the Nakuru air did not always treat her too kindly).

I received a phone call and at the other end was one of the senior clerks at the Regional Assembly. He said they were about to begin an important debate and the President would like me to be there. I told him that was impossible, because my wife was ill in hospital and I had to look after my baby daughter. But if they telephoned after the debate was over and gave me the details I would try to get something into the paper. Then I hung up. A minute later the phone rang again.

'It's Daniel arap Moi here, Mr Dow – I gather you cannot attend the assembly?'

'That's correct – I have to look after my baby daughter.'

'Bring her with you.'

'What – to the Assembly?'

'Yes, we will look after her. There will be no problem. But I really would like you to be here.'

'OK – but I have one or two things to do. What time will the debate start?'

'When you get here.'

So half an hour later Karen and I went to the Rift Valley Regional Assembly to be met by two burly guards who attentively followed me as I perched her car seat on the back of one of the leather chairs, put a finger across my lips to indicate that I wanted silence and took out my notepad.

It was a lively debate. Karen behaved perfectly. The resolution which reaffirmed the *majimbo* stance and again threw down the gauntlet to the Government in Nairobi was approved overwhelmingly and the Right Honourable Assembly members stood to applaud Daniel arap Moi, the man who would be president.

So did Karen, with a big smile on her face and a wilting rusk in one hand.

THE TORTOISE THAT CURES SORE BACKS... AND OTHER ANIMAL STORIES

Karen decided to celebrate the approach of her first birthday by having a dose of the mumps. She did not take too kindly to her temperature going up and had one or two minor convulsions. The doctor decided she would be better off in hospital and she was there for a full week. It was Karen's mumps which led to me coming across a most unusual story which received worldwide coverage.

At the hospital I had a chat with the chief laboratory technologist, Austin Riley, whom I knew well, and he happened to mention that he was having a round of golf in the afternoon.

'Hang on, Austin, you told me you had to give up golf because of your bad back.'

'I did – but my back is OK now.'

'How? You told me you were having to give up golf for ever because that back could not be cured.'

'Well, it is cured now.'

'How?'

'I sat on a tortoise.'

'Pardon?'

'I sat on a tortoise.'

Yes, he sat on a tortoise.

This is the story I wrote as a result of that conversation:

Sore back or lumbago? If the conventional remedies fail, go along to the laboratory of the Nakuru War Memorial Hospital and you'll see a tortoise tied to a tree.

Then, carefully, for a few seconds, sit on it – and the chances are your pains will disappear. It's no hoax – three Europeans, two of them hospital employees, have tried it and got rid of backaches and lumbago.

No doctor has been able to offer an explanation for the amazing cures. Some people say it is an ancient Kikuyu cure, while others credit it to the Zulus of South Africa.

Whatever the source, the chief lab technologist at the hospital, Mr A Riley, is back playing his usual five rounds of golf a week when it seemed at one time as if he might have to give the game up altogether because of his back.

Mr Riley, who keeps a miniature menagerie outside the lab to amuse children, found the tortoise on the golf course and added it to his menagerie.

He told me, 'In the middle of August I had trouble with my back and had to withdraw from the John Stanning tournament. Physiotherapy and exercises helped but I could not get rid of the pain.

'A Kikuyu employee at the hospital told me to sit on the tortoise. He said it was old Kikuyu folklore that if you sat on a tortoise you would cure a backache.

'I scoffed at him, but he kept on at me and eventually, for peace and quiet, I sat on it for a few seconds. That was on Saturday. On Monday I had my first game of golf in a month and I have been playing regularly ever since.

'There is no twinge of pain in my back whatsoever. There is no logical explanation for it, but I am definitely cured.'

The dietician at the hospital, Mrs E Turner, injured her back in a fall. She sat on the tortoise – and the pain disappeared.

The cure, however, is not new to her.

She said, 'I have seen people being cured this way in South Africa. It is an old Zulu trick. It is nothing to do with the level at which you squat down because I've seen tortoises of various sizes used successfully.

'In 1952 a friend of mine in Nakuru had a bad back and could hardly move with it. I told him to sit on the tortoise and, with a smile on his face, he did. His back was cured.'

After Mrs Turner and Mr Riley were cured, Mrs Turner recommended the treatment to her brother-in-law, who was also suffering from a bad back. Mr Turner sat on the tortoise – and his backache disappeared.

He is going to England soon, and yesterday he and some of his African employees were looking for a tortoise on Menengai Crater. Mr Turner is so amazed at the cure that he wants to take a tortoise to England and have it with him all the time.

When I had written the story I persuaded Austin to sit on the tortoise once again so that I could get a photograph of him in the act. Austin duly obliged. True to the Dow photographic tradition, the photographs were out of focus, and I had to go back to Austin the next day and ask him to go through the performance once again. The good-natured Austin obliged and at last I had the story and photograph complete. The *East African Standard* gave it prominent coverage and syndicated the story and photograph throughout the world. The story appeared in various newspapers and journals and I got many requests for more information and photographs. The Nakuru War Memorial Hospital became something of a shrine for back pain sufferers. One elderly couple came unannounced from as far away as Kent and asked to sit on the tortoise. It was all getting out of control and the hospital authorities were more than a little concerned. All that in itself was worthy of a follow-up but I did not want to do anything that would bring more sore backed pilgrims to the hospital so I left the story alone after that.

On subsequent visits to the hospital I would check out Austin's menagerie and look at that world-famous tortoise tied to the tree. I am sure if it had been able to speak it would have looked at me from under that well-worn carapace and said, 'I've now got a helluvah sore back because of all those bastards that have been sitting on it thanks to you.'

Kenya's news stories about animals were not unusual and I had my share of covering them. Some were quite bizarre and, like the tale of the tortoise that could cure core backs and restore that golfing swing, they made headlines all over the world along with my photographs, taken with not a great deal of skill and the use of an old camera which would have been more at home in a museum.

One favourite of mine concerns Rothschild giraffes, a type which was rare in Kenya – they still are – and they were concentrated in the north around a place called Endebess.

There was a danger that they would lose their identity through breeding with other types of giraffe so the East African Wild Life Society decided to shift some of them to another part of Kenya where they could live and breed in comparative isolation.

I heard about this move purely by chance from somebody I knew in the East African Posts and Telegraphs, who said they had been asked to help ensure that the giraffes had a safe journey from Endebess to the Menengai Crater at Nakuru, 160 miles away.

The reason help was needed from the post office was that on this journey the lorry carrying the giraffes would have to pass under telephone wires on their way to Nakuru and this might prove a tall order – decapitation was not the way to save a rare species of giraffe.

Two giraffes, Bahati and Fiona, were chosen to make the first journey. It took ninety minutes and the help of a tranquilliser to get them into wooden boxes which were then winched on to the lorry.

They then set off and the convoy heading south included three post office officials armed with a specially constructed pole. On the forty-five occasions that the giraffes had to pass under telephone wires the officials stood on the back of a lorry and used the wooden poles to push up the wires to ensure that the giraffes passed unscathed underneath.

It was an unusual sight and I had plenty of opportunities to capture it on camera. The story and photographs were on the front page the next day and were used by newspapers all over the world.

It was not a pleasant journey for the giraffes. The safari had a ten-minute stop every hour to give the animals a rest as their constant efforts to maintain balance on the moving vehicle could have strained their hearts.

Bahati and Fiona arrived safely at Menengai Crater. The two which followed on the next trip did not fare as well – seventy miles from their new home they collapsed in the lorry and died of exhaustion. Another pair which made the third and final 160-mile journey arrived safely and that made a total of four left in isolation at Menengai in the hope that they would breed and remain a distinct species.

The outcome that year (1963) was one of mixed fortunes. Fiona, one of the two on that first trip, gave birth six months later, but around the same time one of the giraffes which made the second trip – a bull – had a fatal encounter with a leopard.

I spoke to some Masai tribesmen and they said the giraffe went to the same tree every day to graze and one day a leopard was dozing in the tree. When disturbed it sprang on to the giraffe, holding on to its neck. The giraffe shook it off but had considerable neck injuries and subsequently died.

That left three giraffes who had made that journey plus the new calf and the Rothschild giraffe remains an endangered species in Kenya.

In 1962, a year before Alfred Hitchcock made the famous film, *The Birds*, we had a different version on my home patch.

The invaders were Sudanese diochs, tiny birds which can wipe out entire wheat fields, and in 1962 the breeding conditions in East Africa suited them admirably. They first of all invaded Tanganyika then headed for Kenya. When in flight they darken the sky like locusts and their affect on crops, livelihoods and the economy can be devastating.

Despite the efforts of scientists the only way then to dispose of them was by using gelignite and blowing them to smithereens. The trick was to find out where they would roost at night. When the diochs were out nibbling their way through wheat fields agriculture officials would enter the roost to prepare the trap – drums containing a thirty-gallon mixture of diesel oil and petrol.

By the time the birds reached Njoro, near Nakuru, no fewer than two million diochs had been killed in explosions on four different farms. I interviewed the man who set the traps, East Africa's expert on diochs. He was fanatical about destroying them – years previously they had wiped out his farm in Tanganyika and since then he had killed six million of them.

This time in Njoro he estimated that around 500,000 were feeding away. He had located their roost and set the trap. All we had to do was to wait from a vantage point 300 yards away – the minimum distance for our own safety. I sat with him and his crew and watched as the belly filled little birds weaved and twisted as they approached their base at dusk and finally settled in the trees.

We waited until it was reckoned that they had all returned and the word was given to ignite the fuse. A tremendous explosion lit up the sky and all of a sudden it was raining cooked chicken.

They were falling all over the place and Africans were ready to fill their sacks – the entire roost had been wiped out.

One Saturday morning I got a phone call from the police to tell me that a farmer had been trampled to death by a wounded elephant at Subukia, forty-five miles away. So I grabbed my camera and notebook and set off on what proved to be a precarious journey on a poor road.

I subsequently learned that the farmer saw eight elephants destroying crops on his farm. He fired six shots into a large bull, which made off into the bush.

He tracked it to a neighbour's farm then lost it. He told the neighbour he was going home to get more ammunition and would return to finish the job. When he returned he disappeared into the bush and one shot was heard.

Apparently the elephant had charged the farmer and he had fired one shot at it, hitting it square on the forehead but the elephant kept on charging. The farmer started to run but he caught his foot in a hole and fell while the elephant thundered straight through the bush and on to him.

The farmer was regarded as a first-class shot and had killed elephants before. The fact that seven bullets failed to take this elephant down suggested that the farmer had been using soft-nosed bullets – this was enough to wound the animal severely but not enough to put it down.

I got there hours after the event and by this time a game warden had been called in and had killed the elephant. I decided I wanted a photograph of the downed elephant and tracking it was not difficult because there was a trail of Africans coming in the opposite direction carrying chunks of elephant meat.

By the time I got to the dead elephant there was not really much left to photograph, so I headed back. My walk there had lasted just over an hour and by then it was late afternoon. Most of the Africans had gone and I realised to my horror that I was not sure where I had left my car. And I knew that seven elephants, no doubt more than a little nervous, were still in the area.

I have to record that the next sixty minutes were the scariest of my life. Every movement in the tall grass scared the hell out of me. I remembered that I had left my car beside a stream and when I heard the tinkle of running water I knew I was nearing safety. But to reach safety did I follow the water upstream or downstream? A bit of logic would have helped but I was beyond logic – it does not really mix with near-panic.

It took me an hour and twenty minutes to find my car and I have never been so relieved. I drove home slowly in the dusk to relay my story to Lorna and to get it written for the Monday *East African Standard*.

It made the front page along with another story I had picked up on the Sunday about a local doctor nearly killed by an enraged buffalo while he and his family were on a picnic.

It was never a dull life in Nakuru.

KENYATTA TAMES THE WHITE SETTLERS - AND WRITES THE SCRIPT FOR MANDELA

Nakuru was the unofficial capital of the White Highlands. Its Town Hall had seen many memorable meetings, but none as historic as that held on Monday, 12 August 1963. That was the day that Kenyatta entered the lions' den and emerged conqueror.

The white farmers have long memories and by then thousands were already trekking their way to the Rhodesias and South Africa and further afield because they could not stand the thought of living in a country governed by Africans.

But many others had learned that they had to accept the inevitable and were prepared to give it a go and try to live in a new multiracial Kenya.

There was only one snag. The man who was going to be the first prime minister of an independent Kenya was the hated Jomo Kenyatta, the man said to be behind the Mau Mau and the atrocities and horrors it brought to the country. Memories were still sharp of friends who had been maimed and butchered by the Mau Mau but they remembered that they had stuck it out because Kenya was a British colony and they believed it was going to stay that way. Now they were having to give in to African rule and bow to Kenyatta.

Here he was touring Kenya trying to win friends, being diplomatic and saying all the right things, making the right promises to all races. He was getting the Africans to chant '*harambee*', which was Swahili for 'pulling together' and was meant to be a symbol of unity. Yes, unity against us, was the view of the white farmers, so why should we go along and listen to this evil bastard coming to speak in our own town hall?

That was the mood, that was the setting as hard-bitten white settlers contemplated the arrival of Kenyatta, smirking with victory, to spread the gospel on their patch. They could have stayed at home and ignored him, given him the cold shoulder.

But the farmers had more sense and did not stay at home. This was destiny time.

They had to hear what this man had to say; they had to see this devil in the flesh. More than 300 of them packed into Nakuru Town Hall and I had a prime spot in the press row at the front.

Kenyatta came on stage, smiled and waved his famous fly whisk. Polite applause. He was introduced by the president of the Kenya National Farmers' Union, Lord Delamere, who said there were a number of matters causing farmers a considerable amount of worry and alarm.

There was silence as Kenyatta rose to speak to what was undoubtedly a hostile, sceptical audience.

> We must learn to forgive one another. There is no society of angels, black, brown or white. We are human beings and as such are bound to make mistakes.
>
> If I have done a mistake to you, it is for you to forgive me. If you have done a mistake to me, it is for me to forgive you.
>
> The Africans cannot say the Europeans have done all the wrong and the Europeans cannot say the Africans have done all the wrong.
>
> We are all human beings and, as such, are likely to do wrong. The good thing is to be able to forget and forgive one another. You have something to forget, just as I have.
>
> Kenyatta has no intention of retaliation or looking backwards. We are going to forget the past and look forward. I have suffered imprisonment and detention, but that is gone and I am not going to remember it.
>
> Let us join hands and work for the benefit of Kenya, not for the benefit of one particular community.

The audience was completely stunned. It was undoubtedly a statesmanlike conciliatory speech of the kind they had not expected to hear. When it came to question time they were falling over themselves to politely quiz the Prime Minister. I noted in my diary: 'Today was a big, important one in the history of Kenya – and I was there to cover it. Kenyatta, now, of course, prime minister, spoke to more than 300 European farmers in the Nakuru Town Hall, most of them remembering the horrible Mau Mau which Kenyatta started. Now he was boss – and he made it clear that everything on both sides should be forgotten. I sat in the front row of the press corps and took copious notes. I phoned over more than a column and it was the front page lead the next day. This speech made headlines all over the world. It was a speech which was unique and historic.'

Kenyatta was applauded several times during his speech and at the end of it was given a standing ovation.

That was amazing enough but there was more to come.

When Kenyatta urged them to shout *'harambee'* with him they did so – until then the white settlers had had a derisory attitude to this African chant which was being pushed as a symbol of unity. There was nothing derisory that day – the voices of European farmers shouting *'harambee'* echoed throughout the hall and those listening outside must have shaken their head in disbelief. Kenyatta, the leader to darkness and death, the man who had flirted with Communism, married an Englishwoman, had a bit part in 1935 in *Sanders of the River* alongside the great Paul Robeson and been railroaded into jail and detention by the British Government had put on an impressive performance and conquered the tough white settlers.

He was the man who had first fanned the winds of change that Harold Macmillan warned would sweep through Africa. He wrote the script and set the example for Nelson Mandela.

THE THREAT FROM THE LAND FREEDOM ARMY - AND ROBERT MITCHUM FIGHTS THE MOSQUITOES

That Nakuru meeting was a significant victory for Kenyatta but he still had many more battles on his hands. The dreaded oathing ceremonies were rife throughout the country, land was being seized by squatters and farmers were arming their guards to protect their stock from marauding gangs.

All this was during the run-in to important constitutional talks in London which would pave the way to independence. KADU, the Opposition party, was continuing to push hard for as much autonomy as possible outside of the Kikuyu-dominated Nairobi and in particular in the Rift Valley – of which Nakuru was capital.

During the Emergency the members of Mau Mau had sworn oaths to obey and kill to get their independence. The oaths were of a degrading nature, intended to strip a human being of all his dignity and imbue him with a sense of bravado, immunity and thirst for what was regarded as revenge.

The fact that oath-taking was on the increase again as Kenyatta slowly took the country towards independence was a worrying danger, an unsettling reminder of things past. It seemed that every day I was writing stories about more oath-taking ceremonies, more arrests and more warnings about security risks.

The day after the Nakuru meeting I had another front page lead with a Kenyatta speech, but this time instead of winning over white farmers he was warning his countrymen against taking part in oathing ceremonies.

He stated:

> I want them to stop it or I will face them. In the old days you were taking oaths to be more united and get *uhuru*. Now your Government is here with me, whom you call your leader, the Prime Minister.

There are people who still believe there is some benefit in oathing and making guns in the forest but we shall teach them a lesson.

A week later I travelled to Thomson's Falls to cover a meeting given by the Minister for Home Affairs, Oginga Odinga, a maverick who was sometimes on the right of outrageous but this time he was very much on Kenyatta's side. (And, of course, the late Odinga was the father of Raila Odinga, now making his mark in a different generation of Kenyan politics. He was a member of the Luo tribe, as is the father of US presidential candidate Barack Obama.)

He said that people should cooperate with the Prime Minister and stop taking oaths, and he added: 'Mau Mau oaths were taken and the aim of Mau Mau has been achieved because we have got independence. The work of the oath is finished because there is nobody to fight.'

On the political front I reported that KADU had said they would boycott the pre-independence talks unless the constitution which gave powers to the regions was maintained, clearly a response to Government suggestions that there would be no such thing as regionalisation after independence.

The KADU response was that if this was the case there would be chaos, confusion and disruption, and the man to the fore in demanding that regionalisation be guaranteed was none other than Daniel arap Moi, President of the Rift Valley Regional Assembly (and one-time babysitter organiser for Karen). Regionalisation was certainly not something that he would tolerate years later when he succeeded Kenyatta as president.

Land was a major issue but it was still a difficult time for the farmers who liked what Kenyatta had told them but were having to cope with squatters, stock thefts and constant threats.

Membership of the Land Freedom Army continued to grow. One Nakuru magistrate, Alastair Kneller, described it as a new Mau Mau – he had in front of him fourteen people on Land Freedom Army and firearms charges. One of them, jailed for three years for the unlawful possession of a pistol, said he was told it would be used in the fight against the Europeans or KADU after *uhuru*.

I reported on a massive security sweep in which twenty-four people suspected of being leading members of the Land Freedom Army were arrested. The operation was described as a relentless campaign against dangerous subversive elements who were enemies of the State and the people.

One magistrate sat all day and imposed jail sentences totalling 156 years on forty-five people who admitted being members of the Land Freedom Army. Many who received lighter sentences were old men who claimed they had been forced to take the oath. One man was worried about the fate of his three wives and twenty-three children while he was in prison and another asked if he would be allowed to vote while in prison.

I relayed these quotes in an effort to show that perhaps at the grassroots these so-called threats to the State were simply from people caught up in something outwith their control. I suspected that for the vast majority it made life simpler for them if they agreed to go along with the militants – as with thousands in the days of the Mau Mau – but the growth in membership nonetheless was a clear indication that the die-hard militants were making plans to seize land and drive out the Europeans. It was also basically tribal, with the powerful Kikuyu determined that they would get the bulk of the land and power once independence arrived.

A leader in the *East African Standard* put it this way:

There are doubts and uncertainty which still linger in the minds of many who sincerely want to make their home in Kenya. These are the people who were tremendously cheered and reassured by the Prime Minister's words to them at Nakuru – 'We want you to stay and farm in this country' – and his promise of firm action against stock thieves and other wrongdoers.

This feeling of reassurance has not been seriously shaken but farmers have had an increasingly harassing time in recent weeks. Stock thieving has continued unabated on African as well as European farms and there is mounting pressure from Rift Valley tribes for further land settlement to be rapidly implemented, accompanied by threats of squatting and trouble-making on European farms if no action is taken.

It is true that the Government has had little time since the Nakuru meeting to solve all these problems, preoccupied as it is in other directions, and it can be expected that firm measures will be taken to prevent lawlessness getting out of hand. It is obvious that pressure is going to increase for more settlement schemes.

While many disgruntled farmers fought to keep hold of their land or reluctantly decided to put it on the market and head for a new life in South Africa there were some good news stories and they were always welcome.

One I covered concerned a farmer, A Vidor (we did not seek out Christian names in those days), who was Hungarian-born and had been wanted by the Gestapo when he lived in Vienna just before the war. In 1938 he fled to Kenya and bought 800 acres at Ol Kalau.

He was a successful farmer but, at the age of seventy, decided that it was time to pack up and return to Vienna. There was a willing purchaser – J M Kariuki, a member of the Kenya Parliament and the author of a book called *The Mau Mau Detainee*.

He bought the farm for £11,000, thirty per cent of it being a grant from the British Government. The deal included a herd of pedigree cattle, three houses and three miles of a river stocked with trout.

Both parties were pleased with the deal. I interviewed them both and took a photograph of them on the farm – the photograph made the front page and the story was inside. It was a good example of a peaceful change of land ownership from a European to an African.

That same day I covered a political meeting at which Mr Kariuki spoke to more than 4,000 people. He said that nobody was allowed to go on to European farms and claim that the land was theirs and he urged Europeans not to be frightened by people claiming land because they had no right to do so.

Mr Kariuki was never afraid to air his views and this led to a tragic postscript to my story. Eleven years later Mr Kariuki, by then an even more wealthy Kikuyu politician, was assassinated as Kenya continued to struggle internally with its tribal conflicts. Kariuki was regarded as having been a thorn in the flesh of Jomo Kenyatta's Government because he spoke out against corruption as well as advocating radical wealth and land redistribution.

So the man who had shown the way to compassionate,

sensible land redistribution soon after independence paid the price for constantly airing his views.

As independence approached, Lorna and I had to make decisions about our future. I was twenty-five and my four-year contract expired three months after independence. I had no doubt that I could negotiate another contract but, married with a young child, I was not sure about a safe and secure future in Kenya.

Kenya became independent on 12 December 1963 and my diary entry for 11 December reads:

I am writing this forty-seven minutes before Kenya becomes independent. I will not pretend that it is a joyous occasion; for me there is no joy in seeing the British flag brought down in one of its loveliest and yet disloyal colonies.

The wireless is blaring out the commentary and it is military music at the moment. Now the man who organised Mau Mau, Jomo Kenyatta, becomes prime minister of an independent Kenya. What will happen to the Europeans in this country? Life will not be easy. All the fun and games at the moment are in Nairobi and my part as a reporter is mainly the security angle.

I do not miss the Nairobi side or wish I was there. I do not honestly believe that Kenya will be a safe and happy country but it will not be a Congo. I know independence is inevitable. Britain has not played a fair game with the settlers and I doubt if a new African Government will be fairer.

'I will listen past midnight, not with any trace of excitement. It is, of course, a historic moment but it makes me sad – what else from a patriotic Briton? Not long now – about forty minutes. Goodbye to the wonderful Kenya that Lorna and I know and Karen was born in.

Reading that passage all those years later I detect a streak of jingoism I did not know I had. The views recorded then would certainly not be deemed today as being politically correct, to say the least. But I have always believed that a diary should reflect your views and thoughts at the time of writing in the full knowledge that when read years later they might appear to be passé and out of date.

But, at the age of twenty-five, having first stepped on the shores of Africa at the age of twelve, having been educated there and cut my teeth as a journalist on that great continent I was seeing the country as I knew it come to an end and felt entitled to record my views.

The independence celebrations went off quietly but on my home patch of Nakuru things were starting to hot up, led by none other than Daniel arap Moi. He was president of the Rift Valley Regional Assembly and it was not an organisation which got off to a punctual start.

Its first meeting was scheduled for 8.30 a.m. on Tuesday, 17 December but the meeting did not start until well after 11 and one of the first issues it dealt with was the Rift Valley regional flag which they called the Weeping Kamau. This was clearly defying the Government, which issued a statement warning the Assembly of the dangers of such a move. Mr Daniel arap Moi held a press conference in Nakuru at which he underlined the region's determination to go ahead.

It was a belligerence which was purely tribal – Moi led the Kalenjin tribes and the Government was dominated by Kikuyu. It was as simple as that and if a crystal ball had told me then that Moi would succeed Kenyatta as leader of Kenya I would have thrown it in the bucket.

I know that Moi is not keen to talk about those early days but without doubt he was the man standing up to the Government and many believed there was a real danger of a determined move by the Rift Valley to break away from Nairobi. This did nothing to ease the anxiety of the farming community.

For me the decision had been made.

At the end of my four-year contract I would return home to get myself back on the career ladder in the UK. There was another reason – Lorna did not take too kindly to the Nakuru climate. While she loved the place she was never in the best of health during her three years in Nakuru.

But my last few months in Nakuru were busier than ever. I had taken on the additional role of being the Rift Valley correspondent of the Kenya Broadcasting Corporation – not live broadcasting but supplying a news service. That helped the pocket money immensely.

Uhuru was in the December and we were due to go back to the UK in April once my contract had finished.

Independence had arrived peacefully and life continued as normal. At the Nakuru Theatre the pantomime was *Good King Wencelas* and we enjoyed it. It was the usual babysitting procedure – Karen was in a Moses basket in the back of the car which was parked outside the theatre while we enjoyed the panto inside.

There was a row of cars with sleeping babes inside but there were regular patrols and if a baby was crying they knew where the parents were sitting and word was soon relayed to them. It was simple and efficient and there was no reason in an independent Kenya to think we should change our ways. Yes, on the farms and away from the towns there were concerns about security but it was life as usual in Nakuru.

The news stories were not all about security.

Forty miles south at Naivasha, halfway between Nakuru and Nairobi, they were filming *Mr Moses* starring Robert Mitchum and the delectable Caroll Baker. It was about a quack doctor being the only person who could persuade an African tribe to move before their land is flooded and he leads them to their promised land. It was described by the critics as an adventure spectacle with naïve Biblical parallels. The cast also included Ian Bannen and Alexander Knox.

I'd love to have been there to see the shooting but there was enough happening elsewhere. I did get word, however, that the shooting had been suspended because the film unit were being attacked and harassed by mosquitoes. The film company sent out an SOS to the Pyrethrum Board in Nakuru asking for supplies of mosquito repellent. The Pyrethrum Board was in charge of an insecticide industry which was an important part of Kenya's economy and coming to the rescue of Robert Mitchum and Carroll Baker was good for the publicity business.

It made a good yarn, which I had to check out long distance because I could not spare the time to visit the location. I kept in touch with what was happening at Naivasha in the hope of getting another story or, better still, finding the time to go down there and see Caroll Baker, bites an' all, but no luck. That night we went to the local cinema and saw Bob Hope in *Call Me Bwana* – as my diary said it was about East Africa and he made the film without going near the place. Clearly I admired Caroll Baker for battling the nasty mosquitoes and sampling the realism of filming in East Africa.

I got a telegram from an American magazine offering me 28 dollars – about £9 – for my story on the tortoise that seemed to cure bad backs. That was big money in those days and I did not waste any time in hitting the typewriter.

I covered the Prime Minister opening an agricultural show 150 miles from Nakuru, there was a story about a European farmer being attacked at Molo north of Nakuru but he was not badly injured and I found time to write about volleyball for my weekly sports column.

It was a fairly quiet start to my last year in Africa but there were one or two ominous signs.

In Zanzibar the African Opposition seized power from the ruling Arabs in a swift and well-planned *coup d'état*. They took over control of the police stations and the airport. Snipers were roaming the island and looters were everywhere.

A week later there was a newsflash on the morning radio about an attempted military takeover in Dar es Salaam, where I started my newspaper life. My diary recorded: 'There's big trouble there – Nyerere can't be found. All sorts of rumours are flying around and the wireless has stayed on all day. Following so close on the revolution in Zanzibar it has really shocked everybody we know and there is now that terrible realisation that it could just as easily happen here.'

Two days later my diary stated: 'Nyerere has appeared and made a reassuring broadcast – but I still think the country will never be the same again. And it will take a long time for Europeans in Kenya to get over it.'

It took only two more days for the trouble to spread to Kenya. And it was right on my doorstep.

MUTINY BY THE ARMY – AND A FAREWELL TO AFRICA

The day started with a trip to Naivasha to cover a meeting between Fred Kubai, the Parliamentary Secretary to the Minister for Labour, and a number of farmers who were worried about their future.

Kubai, who had spent some time in detention with Jomo Kenyatta for his part in the Mau Mau uprising, attended a meeting in the house of one of the farmers. He listened intently, took notes and said all the right things.

He told farm labourers that by working hard for the European farmers they would help the Government make a profit. He spoke out against illegal squatting but admitted 'the situation is very serious'.

The situation was to become much more serious that night.

Lorna and I went to the local cinema along with a friend of ours, John McCallum, whose wife was in hospital after having a baby. John was an officer in the King's African Rifles (KAR), who were stationed just down the road at Lanet.

The film we watched was *The Great Escape*, and during the interval – there was always a cinema interval to boost the bar takings – I was approached by an African whom I knew well. He worked for the Government Information Office and he told me that the police and the army were standing by for possible trouble with the King's African Rifles at Lanet and in Nairobi.

It was about 10 p.m. and it had been a long day. We were enjoying *The Great Escape*. So, what the hell, the local reporter and the KAR officer ignored the tip-off and went back into the cinema to see how Steve McQueen was getting on.

We got home just after midnight and very quickly I got a call from a police contact to tell me that the KAR had mutinied at Lanet and that police and army reinforcements were being rushed to the scene.

I dashed into town to find police and army activity everywhere. The police, normally fairly forthcoming with me, were not too cooperative but I managed to get enough information to put together a story.

The mutiny had started about 8.30 on the Friday night, just as we were settling down to watch *The Great Escape*. A group of men broke into the armoury at Lanet and made off with 120 weapons and two boxes of ammunition.

Many other soldiers were dragged out of bed and told to join the uprising. By this time there were more than 200 mutineers, heavily armed, and they were in an ugly mood. The response was swift, and it came from the three RHA, supported by fifty Royal Engineers and a platoon of Gordon Highlanders.

I had enough information to compile my story and I went to a public telephone outside the post office to phone it over to the paper.

The call was taken in Nairobi by another reporter, Peter McDonald, who was acting as a copy-taker because the rush was on to get out a special noon edition on the mutiny. I started to read over my copy and I got to the middle of the second paragraph when a voice interrupted, 'I don't think you can say that, Jim.'

It was Superintendent Jock Bell of the Rift Valley CID. They were monitoring all calls in and out of Nairobi and my on-the-spot story from Nakuru was receiving particular attention. Anything that went to the *East African Standard* would be syndicated worldwide and this was a particularly sensitive time in Kenya, just over a month into independence.

My story got through but only after the police had made the alterations and deletions they wanted.

That was the Saturday morning. Nakuru was sealed off and no other journalist was able to get through. One who did somehow make it from Nairobi with typical indefatigability was *East African Standard* photographer Vic Tomasyan, an old friend.

The two of us went out to where all the action was taking place, managing to avoid a roadblock, and we ducked into a ditch at the side of the road. Around 200 mutineers were holed up in the camp and, despite being warned that force would be met with force, they showed no signs of giving up.

There had already been heavy exchanges of fire and the bullets were still whizzing over the ditch. I had no hesitation in keeping my head down – one soldier had already been killed and a passing African civilian had been wounded.

Then the army started to move in – more than 120 men in fourteen Land Rovers and four armoured cars with an ambulance bringing up the rear. Vic and I looked at this convoy heading for the centre of the activity and into mutineers' territory and instinctively we knew what we were going to do.

We jumped into the back of one of the Land Rovers. The soldiers in it gave us a brief glance and were not perturbed by our arrival. They had other things on their mind.

Ten minutes into the camp were heard a message crackling over the radio: 'One or two arrests, a few surrenders, and lots of people about. We have reached the armoury.'

Just then there were short, sharp bursts of Bren gun fire which seemed to come from the armoury and it was soon all over. We could see mutineers with hands on heads being herded into a compound.

Our Land Rover took us straight to the headquarters of Chief of Staff Brigadier D W Jackson, the main in charge. I expected that we might be in trouble because of our unauthorised use of army transport into what was undoubtedly a danger zone but he greeted us and was happy enough to give us the details we wanted.

He described the mutiny as 'a catching disease' and said it could have led to a flare up of the whole Kenya Army if it had not been controlled quickly. He said the men had consistently refused to obey orders and it had been absolutely essential that the mutiny was finished as quickly as possible.

In all, it had lasted just over seventeen hours, and it certainly added to the tension in Kenya and reinforced my decision to call it a day once our four years were up.

Two months after the mutiny the barracks received an official visit from Jomo Kenyatta, the Prime Minister, when he congratulated the troops on their success in combating shifta bandits who were conducting cattle raids from Somalia but he did not mention the mutiny. But he did make the point that Kenya could not keep calling for help from other countries when in difficulty and had to be able to defend itself.

For me this was the beginning of my last week in Africa and to get to the mutiny scene to cover the visit of the Prime Minister I had to rely on the car being push-started by Lorna – I had not had time to take it to the garage.

My story was phoned over that day by 3 and I found time to take Lorna and Karen to the Oyster Shell, a delightful café and meeting place in the centre of Nakuru. After tea and cakes had been down Lorna and Karen were returned home – I had parked on a slope and did not need a push-start – and at 5.15 I attended the annual meeting of Nakuru Chamber of Commerce.

That gave me another story but I still had to attend a cocktail party given by Nakuru Town Council in honour of trade missions in the town from the Communist-ruled Poland and Yugoslavia. That night Lorna and I went to the cinema and enjoyed *Charade*.

The next day I interviewed some of the trade delegates from Poland and Yugoslavia, finished off my final weekly sports column and at last took my car to the garage to ensure that I was not being pushed around Nakuru.

I'd obviously shown to the Kenya Broadcasting Corporation that there was a lot happening in the Nakuru areas because they decided to send their own reporter to be based in Nakuru and I took time out to brief him on who was who and what was what. In advance I had typed out for him a list of local contacts and their numbers – I certainly was not going to need them again!

Yes, the African wind-down had started. I had by then received our air tickets for the flight home and had cleared my desk on the final day. I took Lorna to the hairdresser but I could not put the notebook away and on the last afternoon fitted in a meeting of Nakuru Town Council and managed to get three stories out of it.

That night we went to the police judo club. They had laid on a farewell do for us and I was presented with a Kenya police shield, which still hangs in my study as I write.

The next day it was down to Nairobi for more farewells, the main one given by my colleagues at the *East African Standard*.

We took the long way home, enjoying stopovers at Athens, Rome and Geneva. We collected our new Ford Cortina at the airport and headed for Edinburgh.

Home at last, with no job, no house but some cash.

I did not want to hang around for long. I saw an advertisement from an editor looking for an experienced reporter. With the job came a house and a car – yes, that's what it was like in the '60s. It was with the *St Neots Advertiser* in Huntingdonshire – I did not have a clue about where St Neots was but it was a job and a house.

We got the job, the house and the car. The car was actually a van and I had to give it to the circulation department every Thursday.

My first assignment was to cover the annual sports day of the Eaton Socon School. I found myself chasing after a wee boy to get his name and address because he had won the egg and spoon race.

A couple of months earlier I had been going in with troops who were quelling a mutiny in Kenya.

I came home that day from the Eaton Socon School sports and sat in the lounge of our newspaper-owned house.

'How was the first day?' asked Lorna.

I shook my head and said, 'Well, it was different. I certainly have a lot of adjusting to do.'

Everything is different from Africa.

The dust of Africa after over forty years is still on the shoes. It's in the hair, under the fingernails, in the nostrils.

You never forget having been into Africa.

Printed in the United Kingdom by
Lightning Source UK Ltd., Milton Keynes
139126UK00001B/20/P